Our Father Knows

Our Father Knows

The Prayer that Jesus Taught

Timothy Matthew Slemmons

First edition

PRINTED IN THE UNITED STATES OF AMERICA
9 8 7 6 5 4 3 2 1

Library of Congress Cataloguing-in-Publication Data

Slemmons, Timothy Matthew
Our Father Knows / Timothy Matthew Slemmons - 1st ed.

ISBN-13: 978-1530033652
ISBN-10: 1530033659

With thanksgiving to God
and in loving memory of

Dr. Daniel Louis Stewart
(1961—2013)

friend of my youth
with whom I professed faith in Jesus Christ,
and whose gift of chalice and paten
I will never forget.

"When you are praying, do not heap up empty phrases as the Gentiles do; for they think that they will be heard because of their many words. Do not be like them, for your Father knows what you need before you ask him."

— Matthew 6:7-8

"And without faith it is impossible to please God, for whoever would approach him must believe that he exists and that he rewards those who seek him."

— Hebrews 11.6

True prayer is done in secret, but this does not rule out the fellowship of prayer altogether, however clearly we may be aware of its dangers. In the last resort it is immaterial whether we pray in the open street or in the secrecy of our chambers, whether briefly or lengthily, in the Litany of the Church, or with the sigh of one who knows not what he should pray for. True prayer does not depend either on the individual or the whole body of the faithful, but solely upon the knowledge that our heavenly Father knows our needs. That makes God the sole object of our prayers, and frees us from a false confidence in our own prayer efforts.

— Dietrich Bonhoeffer

CONTENTS

Acknowledgements

This little book took shape quickly over a four-week interval following the submission of my dissertation proposal (January 2003). The formal (but relatively less formal) calling that occasioned it was an adult Sunday school course at the Woodside Presbyterian Church, Yardley, PA. More formally, I had for some time had it in mind to attempt a thorough consideration of one of the classical catechetical *loci*, these being, the sacraments of baptism and the Lord's Supper, the Ten Commandments and the Great Commandment, the Apostle's Creed, and the Lord's Prayer. Aware that, with possible revisions to the proposal, the dissertation itself, and a related mountain of secondary sources looming, another sliver of daylight as now opened up would not soon recur. Thus, the prospect of a month-long study seemed a providential, if brief, opportunity to sketch out a fresh, first-hand study of the prayer that Jesus taught and offer the fruits of it in face-to-face fellowship with the saints in a congregational setting. I am grateful to the Rev. Doug Hoglund of the Woodside congregation for the invitation, to those who engaged this material with me in the course in question, and to members of the adult Bible study group who took an interest: Clay Hayden, Tom Bartlett, Judy Jones, and Victoria Slemmons.

Among the deficiencies of this study will be the fact that relatively few secondary sources have been consulted and cited. Although a far more thorough investigation thereof had been planned, the exhaustive approach that at first (in my naiveté) seemed warranted was soon abandoned, owing to a lack of sufficient time for absorbing, or even taking sufficient stock of, the available secondary sources; a dawning awareness of the staggering vastness of that literature; and, above all, the necessity of dealing first with the primary (scriptural) sources of the prayer that Jesus taught.

This feature may be, of course, counted among the primary strengths of this study as well, in that it is informed, shaped, and "regulated" (to use the traditional term) by the one source, norm, and authority that stands above all others, and asks what is indeed a great cloud of post-canonical dogmatic, liturgical, and interpretive witnesses to wait patiently until called upon, but with no guarantee that they will be. By virtue of this approach, disciplined via the regulative principle of the Reformed tradition, that is, in a space mostly absent both the great dogmaticians and noisy dabblers, the Spirit was given fresh opportunity to present vital and clarifying insights according the Word's own revelatory terms and connective logic—*sola Scriptura*; thus, it is to the workings of the Word and the Spirit that the chief of these acknowledgements is due. By God's providential grace alone—*sola gratia*—can the rapidity with which these studies came together be explained, not least through a deep hunger for a break from the dissertation. Whether there will be evident here any residue of that inspiration, the reader alone must determine. Yes, your role, dear reader, must also be acknowledged here. But let there be no doubt that, before a word was read by any single reader, this book long ago performed the chief work to which it had been appointed, namely, its work on the author, while its revisions have likewise led me back to the ever-refreshing source of The Lord's Prayer. With simple hope, sincere gratitude, and humble wonder at what the Good Lord may yet do with it, here it is offered humbly and with no greater aspiration than that it may stand as an artifact of this instance of edification in the school of the Spirit.

— TMS
"Mamre"
Dubuque, IA
Lent, AD 2016

FOREWORD

Among the great confessional statements of the Reformed tradition, *The Second Helvetic Confession* (1561) looms large indeed. Penned by the Swiss Reformer Heinrich Bullinger, it was originally intended to be attached to his last will and testament to the church in Zürich, where he had succeeded Ulrich Zwingli as pastor. In Chapter XXV of that confession, Bullinger wrote:

> The Lord enjoined his ancient people to exercise the greatest care that young people, even from infancy, be properly instructed. Moreover, he expressly commanded in his law that they should teach them, and that the mysteries of the sacraments should be explained. Now since it is well known from the writings of the Evangelists and apostles that God has no less concern for the youth of his new people, when he openly testifies and says: "Let the children come to me; for to such belongs the kingdom of heaven" (Mark 10:14), the pastors of the churches act most wisely when they early and carefully catechize the youth, laying the first grounds of faith, and faithfully teaching the rudiments of our religion by expounding the Ten Commandments, the Apostles'

> Creed, the Lord's Prayer, and the doctrine of the sacraments, with other such principles and chief heads of our religion. Here let the Church show her faith and diligence in bringing the children to be catechized, desirous and glad to have her children well instructed.[1]

Bullinger's description of the pastor's and the Church's responsibility for positive indoctrination was certainly issued in very different times and on a very different landscape — geographically, sociologically, ecclesiastically — than our own, but for all the history that has elapsed since then, for all the kingdoms that have risen and fallen, the rudiments, the principles, and the chief topics of the Christian faith have not. Another major difference is that, in recent generations, children, youth, young adults, and even older adults in staggering numbers have either missed, avoided, or been deprived of solid catechesis in a way that would have seemed unthinkable, especially in the latter centuries that popularly constitute the former Christendom, from Constantine to Kierkegaard.

All of this is simply by way of introduction to the following study on The Lord's Prayer, which is not here pitched to the very young, but to adults who are active in the faith and to pastors who may be (hopefully sooner rather than later) coming to terms with the need to once again "faithfully teach the rudiments" according to the classical *loci* addressed by the creedal and catechetical traditions of the church.

As stated above in the "Acknowledgments," this study focusses on The Lord's Prayer by way of scripture itself and not primarily by way of subsequent tradition. The reference to Bullinger here is simply a reminder of the vital task to which pastors, other Christian teachers, and parents are called. Neither are the relevant excerpts from the Presbyterian and Reformed confessions included here for any reason other than the reader's convenience. They are placed at the end of each chapter, not at the beginning, so as to exemplify the various ways in which the church has summarized the significance of each petition under consideration. But they are held at bay until the scriptures have been investigated. It is left to the reader to determine how closely the findings of each chapter correspond to the confessional excerpts. Such a determination has not been the aim of this study.

Were this biblical study to be expanded to address the vast, groaning shelves of secondary literature on The Lord's Prayer, it would be necessary, first, to clearly attribute this abundance to the fact that "*the* Prayer" figures prominently among the basics that every pastor of every generation in the Christian era has been called to and should teach; second, to absolve such a study (as well as the reader) of the responsibility for surveying the entirety of the genre; and finally, to identify the most important—the best of the best—and (to a lesser extent) identify a few of the more popular and contemporary treatments from which the reader would benefit. Again, without promising any treatment of the same in the pages that follow, the third of these tasks would narrow the field to selected sources "for further reading," which are listed in more or less chronological order. Any one of these sources could well supplement the present study, while together they would undoubtedly serve as an excellent foundation for a study of the history of interpretation of The Lord's Prayer, a study that would doubtless reveal far greater consistency than innovation.

Meanwhile, since in the course of this study a number of the Lord's other instructions regarding prayer do arise, it seemed fitting at the time the class was first conducted to include a prayer composed of and informed by these passages that, owing to the comparative frequency with which the Lord's Prayer is offered in worship and the relative neglect from which the others suffer, invite greater attention to them and more frequent and faithful use, even where the subject matter is mysterious, their content daunting. This then is by way of explanation of the "Eschatological Postscript" that appears at the conclusion of this study.

For Further Reading

CHURCH FATHERS:

Tertullian, "On Prayer," in *Ante-Nicene Fathers, Volume 3: Latin Christianity: Its Founder Tertullian I. Apologetic; II. Anti-Marcion; III. Ethical, 2nd Printing*, eds. Roberts and Donaldson (Peabody, MA: Hendrickson, 1999), 681-691; esp. 682-684.

Cyprian, "Treatise IV, On the Lord's Prayer," in *Ante-Nicene Fathers, Volume 5: Hippolytus, Cyprian, Caius, Novatian, Appendix, 2nd Printing*, eds. Roberts and Donaldson (Peabody, MA: Hendrickson, 1999), 447-457.

"**The Teaching of the Twelve Apostles**," in *Ante-Nicene Fathers, Volume 7: Lactantius, Venantius, Asterius, Victorinus, Dionysius, Apostolic Teaching and Constitutions, 2 Clement, Early Liturgies, 2nd Printing*, eds. Roberts and Donaldson (Peabody, MA: Hendrickson, 1999), 369-383, esp. 379; or "**The Didache**" (8:1-2), in *The Apostolic Fathers, Second Edition*, trans. by J. B. Lightfoot and J. R. Harmer; ed. Michael W. Holmes (Grand Rapids: Baker Books, 1956), 246-249; esp. 258-259; see also a brief but important passage in "**Constitutions of the Holy Apostles**," in *Ante-Nicene Fathers, Volume 7: Lactantius, Venantius, Asterius, Victorinus, Dionysius, Apostolic Teaching and Constitutions, 2 Clement, Early Liturgies, 2nd Printing*, eds. Roberts and Donaldson (Peabody, MA: Hendrickson, 1999), Book III, Chapter XVIII, 431-32.

Augustine, *The Lord's Sermon on the Mount: Ancient Christian Writers* 5, trans. Jepson (Mahwah, NJ: Paulist Press, 1948) 9, 103-127, 197; and *Confessions and Enchiridion: The Library of Christian Classics, Volume 7*, ed. Albert Cook Outler (Philadelphia: Westminster Press, 1955); see *Enchiridion*, pp. 339ff., 381-383, 407-408.

REFORMERS:

Martin Luther, "The Large Catechism" (1529), in *The Book of Concord: The Confessions of the Evangelical Lutheran Church*, ed. Kolb and Wengert (Minneapolis: Fortress Press, 2000), 377-480; esp. 440-456; see also Gary Neal Hansen, "Chapter 2: Praying with Martin Luther: The Lord's Prayer," in *Kneeling with Giants: Learning to Pray with History's Best Teachers* (Downers Grove, IL: InterVarsity Press, 2012).

John Calvin, *Institutes of the Christian Religion 2: The Library of Christian Classics, Volume 21*, trans. Ford Lewis Battles; ed. John T.McNeill (Philadelphia: Westminster Press, 1960) 3.20.34-49; 897-917; also I. John Hesselink, *Calvin's First Catechism: A Commentary, Featuring Ford Lewis Battle's translation of the* 1538 Catechism: *Columbia Series in Reformed Theology* (Louisville: Westminster John Knox Press, 1997), 27-33; Elsie Anne McKee, "John Calvin's Teaching on The Lord's Prayer," in *The Lord's Prayer: Perspectives for Reclaiming Christian Prayer*, ed. Daniel L. Migliore (Grand Rapids: Eerdmans, 1998).

John Knox, "A Treatise on Prayer," in *The Select Practical Writings of John Knox* (Edinburgh: Banner of Truth Trust, 2011), pp. 1-26.

Hugh Latimer, *Sermons* (London: J. M. Dent & Sons, 1906; New York: E. P. Dutton, 1906).[2] One the seven sermons is available in *Selected Sermons of Hugh Latimer,* ed. Allan G. Chester (Charlottesville: Published for the Folger Shakespeare Library Washington, by University of Virginia Press, 1968); see "First Sermon on the Lord's Prayer" (1552), 158-174.

John Bradford, "Godly Meditations on the Lord's Prayer," in *The Writings of John Bradford, Volume 1* (Edinburgh: The Banner of Truth Trust, 1979).

Zacharias Ursinus, *Commentary on the Heidelberg Catechism*, trans. and ed. G. W. Willard (Grand Rapids: Eerdmans, 1956) 619-659.

PURITANS AND PIETISTS:

Thomas Watson, *A Body of Practical Divinity in a Series of Sermons on The Shorter Catechism, to which is appended Selected Sermons on Various Subjects together with The Art of Divine Contentment, and Christ's Various Fulness* (Glasgow, Edinburgh, and London: Blackie & Son, 1858); see esp. 337-544.[3]

John Wesley, *The Works of John Wesley, Bicentennial Edition, Volume 1: Sermons I: 1-33, ed.* Albert Cook Outler (Nashville: Abingdon, 1984); see "Sermon 26."[4]

Johann Arndt, "Of Inward Prayer, and Of the True Use of the Lord's Prayer," in *True Christianity*, Book III, Chapter XIX. [NB: This classic, including the recommended chapter, is available in a number of reprint editions, but it is *not* among the selections in the widely available volume, edited by Peter Erb, in the *Classics of Western Spirituality* series.][5]

MODERNITY AND NEO-ORTHODOXY:

E. M. Bounds, *The Complete Works of E. M. Bounds on Prayer, Prince Press Edition* (Peabody, MA: Hendrickson Publishers, 2002), 268-69.

Elizabeth Wordsworth, *Thoughts on the Lord's Prayer* (London: Longmans, Green, 1898).

A. J. Worlledge, *Prayer: Oxford Library of Practical Theology, Second Edition* (London, New York, Bombay: Longmans, Green, and Co., 1902).

Karl Barth, et al. *Prayer: 50th Anniversary Edition* (Louisville, KY: Westminster John Knox Press, 2002); see also "Chapter Five: Prayers of Petition," in Deborah van Deusen Hunsinger, *Pray without Ceasing: Revitalizing Pastoral Care* (Grand Rapids: Eerdmans, 2006)

Dietrich Bonhoeffer, et al., "Chapter Six: The Sermon on the Mount," in *Dietrich Bonhoeffer Works 4: Discipleship* (Minneapolis: Fortress Press, 2001), esp. 146-168.

Walter Lüthi, *The Lord's Prayer: An Exposition*, trans. Kurt Schoenenberger (Edinburgh and London: Oliver and Boyd, 1961).

Gardiner M. Day, *The Lord's Prayer: An Interpretation* (Greenwich, CT: Seabury Press, 1954).

Walter Rauschenbusch, *A Rauschenbusch Reader: The Kingdom of God and the Social Gospel, 1st ed.*, ed. Benson Y. Landis (New York: Harper, 1957).

Jean-Jacques von Allmen, *Worship: Its Theology and Practice* (New York: Oxford University Press, 1965), 157-171.

Georg F. Vicedom, *A Prayer for the World: The Lord's Prayer, A Prayer for Mission* (St. Louis: Concordia Pub. House, 1967).

Carmine Di Sante, *Jewish Prayer: The Origins of the Christian Liturgy* (Mahwah, NJ: Paulist Press, 1991), 13-23; and "The Our Father (Lord's Prayer) in Light of the Jewish B^{e}rekah," in Rober Webber, ed., *The Complete Library of Christian Worship, Volume I: The Biblical Foundations of Christian Worship* (Nashville, TN: Star Song, 1993) 142-144.

Alexander Schmemann, *Our Father*, trans. Alexis Vinogradov (Crestwood, NY: St. Vladimir's Seminary Press, 2001).

Contemporary Sources:

N. T. Wright, *The Lord and His Prayer* (Grand Rapids: Eerdmans, 1996).

Stanley Hauerwas and William H. Willimon, *Lord, Teach Us: The Lord's Prayer & the Christian Life* (Nashville: Abingdon, 1996).

H. Stephen Shoemaker, *Finding Jesus in His Prayers* (Nashville: Abingdon Press, 2004).

William J. Carl, III, *The Lord's Prayer for Today* (Louisville: Westminster John Knox Press, 2006).

J. I. Packer, *Praying the Lord's Prayer* (Wheaton, IL: Crossway, 2007).

R. C. Sproul, *The Prayer of the Lord* (Lake Mary, FL: Reformation Trust Publishing, 2009).

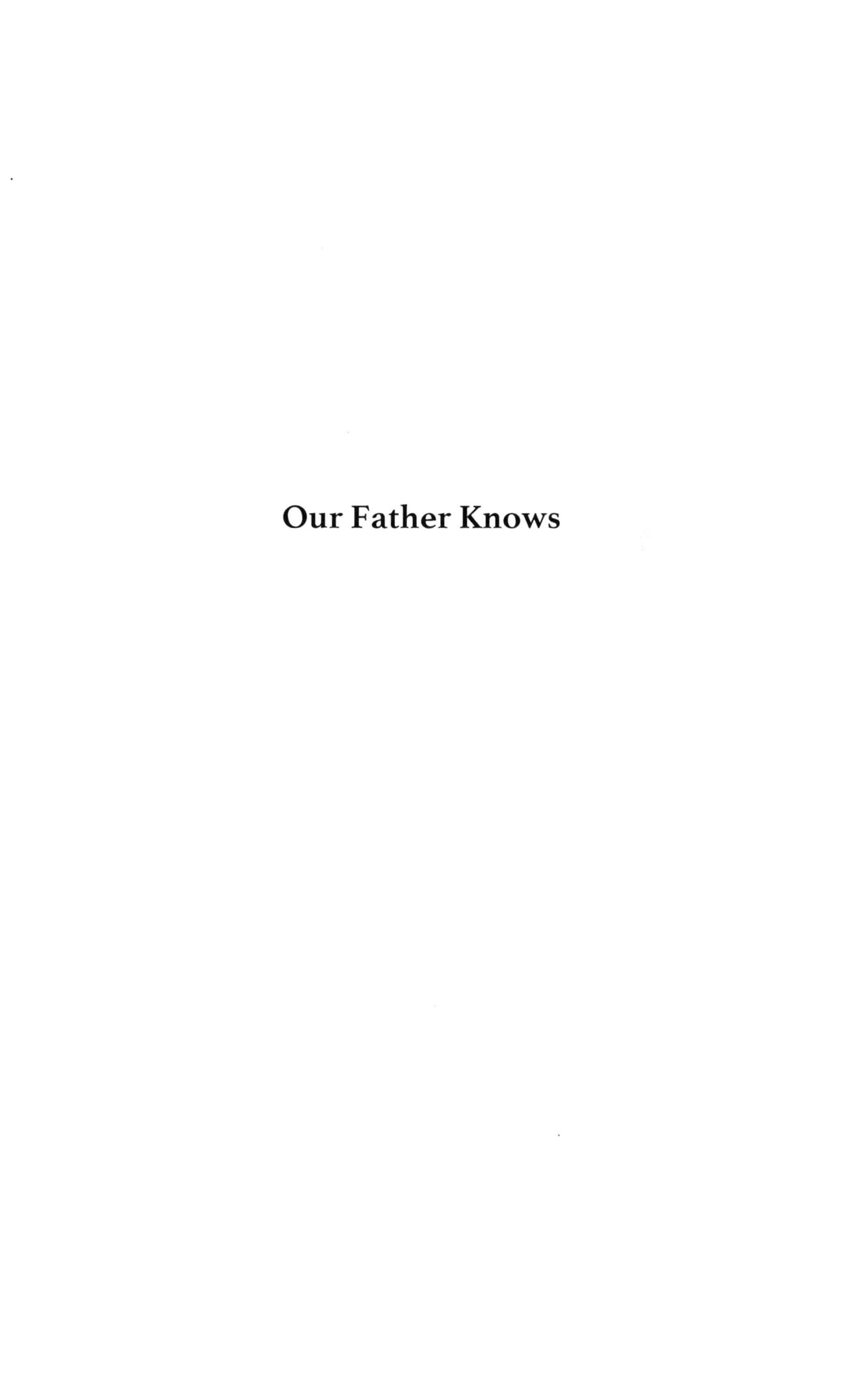

Our Father Knows

Introduction

The Lord's Prayer as we know it derives from two primary biblical sources, namely, from the Sermon on the Mount, found in the Gospel of Matthew (5–7) and from a chapter in the Gospel of Luke that begins quite pastorally (10:38–11:13), but which sees Jesus encountering increased opposition and eventually going on the attack by denouncing the Pharisees and the lawyers, six times saying to them: "Woe to you!" Certainly Luke's version is less well known. One reason for this may be the fact that in Luke, we do not find the phrase, known as the third petition, which asks of the Father, "thy will be done, on earth as it is in heaven" (Matt 6:10), even though, later on, in his prayer in the Garden of Gethsemane, Jesus offers up just such a petition in his moment of greatest testing: "Father, if you are willing, remove this cup from me; yet, not my will but yours be done" (Luke 22:42). Another reason why the Lukan version is less well known, however, may be the fact that, while this teaching on prayer occurs, in unsolicited fashion, at roughly geometric center of the Matthean Sermon on the Mount, in Luke, the disciples literally asked for it: "He was praying in a certain place, and after he had finished, one of his disciples said to him, 'Lord, teach us to pray, as John taught his disciples'" (Luke 11:1). Remarkably, while the setting in Luke depicts Jesus functioning as teacher, the same chapter ends with a strong denunciation of the teachers of the law, who should have been teaching such things, for Jesus says they possess "the key to knowledge," indeed, they "have taken it away," but they neither use it in order to enter themselves, nor do they allow others to enter (11:52), enter into knowledge, presumably. They are not so much like present day attorneys. Their task is, or should be, theological instruction, and their disposition one of prayer and faith. They are those entrusted with preserving, interpreting, and expounding upon the scriptures. In other words, they are like a minister who, were such a thing possible, forgets to pray, neglects the scriptures, refuses to teach Sunday school, fails even to show up for Sunday worship, and when he does, chases everyone away. Perhaps, then, we prefer the version in Matthew to that found in Luke, not only because it is more complete, but because we — we ministers anyway — do not wish to encounter the Jesus of Luke 11! In fact, we are unlikely to do so, since the *Revised Common Lectionary* never ventures beyond v. 13 of that abrasive chapter.

Nevertheless, for the purposes of this study, we will focus on the more complete version of The Lord's Prayer as found in Matthew, all the while keeping Luke 11 in view as our incentive to do our work well, to discover what it means to use the key of knowledge and to enter in a manner pleasing to our Lord who entrusted this prayer to us, not only for our frequent use, but for our deep consideration and our thorough understanding.

It is worth noting, though, that another important extra-canonical source contains a version of The Lord's Prayer that is quite similar to the one found in the Gospel of Matthew. *The Didache* is an early Christian source, discovered in Constantinople and published in 1883. Its title means *the teaching* (of the apostles). In addition to its doctrine of the two ways, proscriptions against various sins, and warnings against false teachings, *The Didache* is an important liturgical source regarding the practice of baptism, the Lord's Supper, fasting, and prayer, including The Lord's Prayer (8:2) and containing the instruction that it be prayed three times each day (8:3).[6] The early church father Cyprian, who saw the prayer as "a compendium of the heavenly doctrine," added two times (at sunrise and sunset) for a total of five daily recitations, while Augustine, less legalistically, simply stated that no day should pass without the Christian praying The Lord's Prayer. Tertullian, like Cyprian, considered the prayer a summary of Christian teaching on the faith and morals.[7] [8]

➢ *The Setting of the Prayer in the Sermon on the Mount* (Matthew 5–7)

Much can be said about the quintessentially Christian sermon at the heart of which we find The Lord's Prayer. The Sermon on the Mount spans three chapters of Matthew's gospel (5–7), and a somewhat more precise threefold division (including preamble) reveals that The Lord's Prayer indeed lies at or very near the geometric center of the sermon's middle section.[9]

Introduction (5:1-20)	The Beatitudes and Preamble
I. (5:21-48)	The Higher Righteousness I (Six Antitheses)
II. (6:1-18)	The Higher Righteousness II
A. (6:1-8)	almsgiving and prayer (in secret), and the warning against babbling prayer
B. (6:9-13)	**The Lord's Prayer**
C. (6:14-18)	The forgiveness of sins; fasting in secret
III. (6:19-7:11)	The Two Kingdoms Contrasted
A. (6:19-24)	earthly v. heavenly treasure; one master
B. (6:25-34)	seek first the kingdom of God and his righteousness
C. (7:1-11)	Prohibition against judging, profanation (giving what is holy to dogs/swine), courage to pray ("ask, ... seek, ... knock")
Conclusion (7:12-29)	The Golden Rule, The Narrow Gate, Concluding Admonitions

Delivered at the inception of his earthly ministry, this sermon, the first of five lengthy discourses in the gospel of Matthew (5–7; 10; 13; 18; 24–25), conveys the essence of Christian teaching concerning the Kingdom of heaven, and it is spoken by none other than Christ, the King himself (2:1; 25:31-46; 27:11, 29, 37; 28:16).

Many consider the beatitudes, with which the Sermon on the

Mount begins, to be a positive restatement or a recapitulation of the Ten Commandments (Exod 20; Deut 5) in the New Testament. Even though as the Christ, Jesus is far more than a prophet, here he is seen as standing in the tradition of Moses, through whom God gave the Law (Torah) to Israel. In the Gospel of John, Jesus is three times described as "the prophet," that is, the prophet like Moses (1:45; 6:14; 7:40), a prophet who is expected because Moses himself prophesied at his departure, that: "The LORD your God will raise up for you a prophet like me from among your own people; you shall heed such a prophet" (Deut 18:15). All four gospels speak of Jesus' manifest authority. Indeed, at the conclusion of the Sermon on the Mount, Matthew tells us that "he taught them as one having authority, and not as their scribes" (Matt 7:29). In the sermon itself, one clear indicator of Jesus' authority is the way in which he says antithetically, no less than six times, "You have heard that it was said, ..." (Matt 5:21, 27, [31], 33, 38, 43) "but I say to you ..." (5:22, 28, 32, 34, 39, 44). In each case, he is not only restating the law, but he is raising the stakes, stating the requirements of the law as the highest ideal, aiming for what Ulrich Luz terms, the "higher righteousness." Nevertheless, he also states quite clearly that he has not come "to abolish the law or the prophets, but to fulfill" them (5:17). Thus, we have every reason to examine the prayer at heart of this sermon, that is, The Lord's Prayer, with the tablets of the Law and their perfect fulfillment in view.

You will recall that the Ten Commandments consist of two tablets, the first being a tablet of four commandments corresponding to our conduct toward God (Exod 20:2-11), and the other corresponding to our conduct toward our neighbor (Exod 20:12-17). Thus, when Jesus is asked, "What is the greatest commandment?" (Matt 22:36), he replies with one that summarizes the first tablet of the law in terms of the thoroughgoing love we are to have for God (Deut 6:4-5), and with another that summarizes the second tablet in terms of the love which we are to show to our neighbor (Lev 19:18b): "'You shall love the Lord your God with all your heart, and with all your soul, and with all your mind.' This is the greatest and first commandment. And a second is like it: 'You shall love your neighbor as yourself'" (Matt 22:37-39). Likewise, in The Lord's Prayer, we find a similar structure, corresponding to our duties to God and to our neighbor. As we shall see, the first three petitions pertain to the Father, each one ending in rhyming fashion with the Greek genitive pronoun *thy* or *your* [σου], while the last three petitions pertain to *us*.

But before we examine in more detail the structure of the prayer, which Lockyer (citing Burgess and Proudlove) categorized as an "index prayer,"[10] let us look more closely at its setting in the middle chapter of the sermon (Matt 6) and consider the nature of prayer itself.

➢ *The Teaching on Prayer: Motivation and Cryptic Secrecy* (Matthew 6:1-8)

Three antithetical statements lay the groundwork for the prayer, which distinguish improper motivation from the proper way to do righteous deeds (6:1). These antitheses concern: (1) almsgiving (6:2-4), (2) the conspicuousness of prayer (6:5-6), and (3) the brevity, simplicity, and order of one's prayers (6:7-8). The first two statements urge a literally "cryptic" secrecy [ἐν τῷ κρυπτῷ], in contrast to attention-seeking motivation. The final statement offers the intimate assurance that our heavenly Father already knows what we need before we ask, thus, we are not to think we can wrest provisions by badgering God or babbling until he gives in. Note the causal statements italicized below:

> Beware of practicing your piety before others *in order to* be seen by them; *for* then you have no reward from your Father in heaven.
>
> So whenever you give alms, do not sound a trumpet before you, as the hypocrites do in the synagogues and in the streets, *so that* they may be praised by others. Truly I tell you, they have received their reward. But when you give alms, do not let your left hand know what your right hand is doing, *so that* your alms may be done in secret; *and* your Father who sees in secret will reward you.
>
> And whenever you pray, do not be like the hypocrites; for they love to stand and pray in the synagogues and at the street corners, *so that* they may be seen by others. Truly I tell you, they have received their reward. But whenever you pray, go into your room and shut the door and pray to your Father who is in secret; *and* your Father who sees in secret will reward you.
>
> When you are praying, do not heap up empty phrases as the Gentiles do; for they think that they will be heard *because of* their many words. Do not be like them, *for* your Father knows what you need before you ask him (6:1-8).

The prohibition against the public display of one's righteous deeds is not absolute, but is qualified by the phrase "*so that* they may be praised/seen by others" (vv. 2, 5). We are not to *parade* our piety, but it is no disaster if others happen to witness a prayer that proceeds from the proper motivation.

There is also a clear sense in which the cryptic or secretive manner in which we are told to go about giving alms and offering prayers is itself an act of faith in God, a way of entrusting God alone with the facts of the case we set before him. In the case of almsgiving, it may be that the recipient of your gift stands in need not only of the gift itself but also of the hope that a delightful and apparently miraculous windfall may inspire. In the case of secret prayer, it may well be that there are those who should not overhear the petition; more importantly, however, to offer your prayer in secret ensures the petition has been wholly entrusted to the Heavenly Father and to no one else. This ensures *your* delight and *your* upbuilding in faith when *you* see God's response to your request, upon receipt of your "reward." Likewise, it guarantees that the righteous acts of giving and praying are not done to assure yourself of your own piety, but to derive your assurance wholly from God who honors such prayer and "will reward you" (v. 6).

This admonition to secrecy must not be misunderstood or misused. It certainly must not be taken as attributing any magical power to the prayer, despite the subsequent rendering of the Greek word κρυπτὸς with the Latin words *absconditus* and *occultus*, both of which simply mean *hidden from view*. Nevertheless, the early church did at times regard The Lord's Prayer as insider information, even a closely guarded mystery or secret, to be taught only to the initiated, to the newly baptized upon their emergence from the waters of rebirth and spoken by them as their first prayer in the kingdom of heaven as children of God.[11]

This element of secrecy appears perhaps slightly more understandable in light of two of the three ways in which the prayer has traditionally been interpreted,[12] namely, *dogmatically* (as a summary of Christian doctrine) and *eschatologically* (with emphasis on the *eschaton* and the *parousia* of Christ, his reappearing or second coming, with the final consummation of the approaching, but now hidden, kingdom). Viewed as doctrine, it is quite likely that the prayer was considered holy, and thus counted among the pearls not to be cast before swine (Matt 7:6). As eschatology, the prayer may be seen as subverting the earthly kingdom of the present age, or conspiring against the rule of the despised master (6:24). The idea of secrecy surrounding The Lord's Prayer makes far less sense when the prayer is reduced to strictly *ethical* terms. For while the prayer certainly bear its radical ethical implications, such a moral reading thereof does not offer a sufficient view of its depths or its importance for Christian faith and hope and love (1Cor 13:1-13). But it is not altogether surprising that the more widely known the prayer has become, the more the popular understanding of it has been boiled down to mere ethics.

But let us allow three confessional statements to elaborate on the nature of prayer generally, each of which does so as a means of approaching The Lord's Prayer and explaining it more explicitly. The relevant portions of these three confessional statements from the Presbyterian *Book of Confessions* — *The Heidelberg Catechism*, *The Westminster Shorter Catechism*, and *The Westminster Larger Catechism* —

will be supplied at the end of each section of this study. It is not my aim to interpret, analyze, critique, or defend these confessions, but simply to ensure the reader has them at hand, in order to supplement, guide, and referee the discussion as needed.

***I. The Heidelberg Catechism* (HC) [LORD'S DAY 45]**

Q.116. Why is prayer necessary for Christians?

A. Because it is the chief part of the gratitude which God requires of us, and because God will give his grace and Holy Spirit only to those who sincerely beseech him in prayer without ceasing, and who thank him for these gifts.

Q.117. What is contained in a prayer which pleases God and is heard by him?

A. First, that we sincerely call upon the one true God, who has revealed himself to us in his Word, for all that he has commanded us to ask of him. Then, that we thoroughly acknowledge our need and evil condition so that we may humble ourselves in the presence of his majesty. Third, that we rest assured that, in spite of our unworthiness, he will certainly hear our prayer for the sake of Christ our Lord, as he has promised us in his Word.

Q.118. What has God commanded us to ask of him?

A. All things necessary for soul and body which Christ the Lord has included in the prayer which he himself taught us.

Q.119. What is the Lord's Prayer?

A. "Our Father who art in heaven, hallowed be thy name. Thy kingdom come, thy will be done, on earth as it is in heaven. Give us this day our daily bread; and forgive us our debts, as we also have forgiven our debtors; and lead us not into temptation, but deliver us from evil, for thine is the kingdom and the power and the glory, forever. Amen" (*BOC*, HC 4.116-119).

***II. Westminster Shorter Catechism* (WSC)**

Q.98. What is prayer?

A. Prayer is an offering up of our desires unto God (Ps 62:8; 10:17), *for things agreeable to his will* (1John 5:14; Matt 26:39; John 6:38), *in the name of Christ* (John 16:23), *with confession of our sins* (Dan 9:4), *and thankful acknowledgment of his mercies* (Phil 4:6).

Q.99. What rule hath God given for our direction in prayer?

A. The whole Word of God is of use to direct us in prayer (2Tim 3:16; 1John 5:14)*; but the special rule of direction is that form of prayer which Christ taught his disciples, commonly called "the Lord's Prayer"* (Matt 6:9) (*BOC*, WSC 7.098-099).

***III. Westminster Larger Catechism* (WLC)**

Q.178. What is prayer?

A. Prayer is an offering up of our desires unto God (Ps 62:8), *in the name of Christ* (John 16:23-24), *by the help of his Spirit* (Rom 8:26), *with confession of our sins* (Dan 9:4; Ps 32:5-6), *and thankful acknowledgment of his mercies* (Phil 4:6).

Q.179. Are we to pray unto God only?

A. *God only being able to search the heart* (1Kings 8:39; Acts 1:24; Rom 8:27), *hear the requests* (Ps 65:2), *pardon the sins* (Mic 7:18), *and fulfill the desires of all* (Ps 145:16, 19), *and only to be believed in* (2Sam 22:32; John 14:1), *and worshiped with religious worship* (Matt 4:10); *prayer, which is a special part thereof* (1Cor 1:2), *is to be made by all to him alone, and to none other* (Luke 4:8; Isa 42:8; Jer 3:23).

Q.180. What is it to pray in the name of Christ?

A. *To pray in the name of Christ is, in obedience to his command, and in confidence on his promises, to ask mercy for his sake* (John 14:13-14; Dan 9:17): *not by bare mentioning of his name* (Luke 6:46; Matt 7:21); *but by drawing our encouragement to pray, and our boldness, strength, and hope of acceptance in prayer, from Christ and his mediation* (Heb 4:14-16; 1John 5:13-15).

Q.181. Why are we to pray in the name of Christ?

A. *The sinfulness of man, and his distance from God by reason thereof, being so great, as that we can have no access into his presence without a mediator, and there being none in heaven or earth appointed to, or fit for, that glorious work but Christ alone, we are to pray in no other name but his only* (John 14:6; Eph 3:12; 1Tim 2:5; John 6:27; Col 3:17; Heb 7:25-27; 13:15).

Q.182. How doth the Spirit help us to pray?

A. *We not knowing what to pray for as we ought, the Spirit helpeth our infirmities, by enabling us to understand both for whom, and what, and how prayer is to be made; and by working and quickening in our hearts (although not in all persons, nor at all times in the same measure) those apprehensions, affections, and graces, which are requisite for the right performance of that duty* (Rom 8:26; Ps 10:17; 80:18; Zech 12:10).

Q.183. For whom are we to pray?

A. We are to pray for the whole church of Christ upon earth (Eph 6:18; Ps 28:9), *for magistrates* (1Tim 2:1-2), *and ministers* (2Thess 3:1; Col 4:3), *for ourselves* (Gen 32:11), *our brethren* (Jas 5:15; 2Thess 1:11), *yea, our enemies* (Matt 5:44), *and for all sorts of men living* (1Tim 2:1-2), *or that shall live hereafter* (John 17:20; 2Sam 7:29); *but not for the dead.*[13]

Q.184. For what things are we to pray?

A. We are to pray for all things tending to the glory of God (Matt 6:9), *the welfare of the church* (Pss 51:18; 122:6), *our own* (Matt 7:11) *or others' good* (Ps 125:4; 1Thess 5:23; 2Thess 3:16); *but not for anything that is unlawful* (1John 5:14; Jas 4:3).

Q.185. How are we to pray?

A. We are to pray with an awful apprehension of the majesty of God (Ps 33:8; 95:6), *and deep sense of our own unworthiness* (Gen 18:27; Ps 144:3), *necessities* (Ps 86:1; Luke 15:17-19), *and sins* (Ps 130:3; Luke 18:13); *with penitent* (Ps 51:17; Zech 12:10-14), *thankful* (Phil 4:6; 1Thess 5:8), *and enlarged hearts* (Ps 81:10; Eph 3:20-21); *with understanding* (1Cor 14:15), *faith* (Heb 10:22; Jas 1:6), *sincerity* (Heb 10:22; Ps 17:1; 145:18; John 4:24), *fervency* (Jas 5:16), *love* (1Tim 2:18; Matt 5:23-24), *and perseverance* (Eph 6:18), *waiting upon him* (Mic 7:7) *with humble submission to his will* (Matt 26:39).

Q.186. What rule hath God given for our direction in the duty of prayer?

A. The whole Word of God is of use to direct us in the duty of praying (2Tim 3:16-17; 1John 5:14)*; but the special rule of direction is that form of prayer which our Saviour Christ taught his disciples, commonly called, "the Lord's Prayer"* (Matt 6:9-13; Luke 11:2-4).

Q.187. How is the Lord's Prayer to be used?

A. The Lord's Prayer is not only for direction, as a pattern according to which we are to make other prayers; but may be also used as a prayer so that it be done with understanding, faith, reverence, and other graces necessary to the right performance of the duty of prayer (Matt 6:9; Luke 11:2).

Q.188. Of how many parts doth the Lord's Prayer consist?

A. The Lord's Prayer consists of three parts: a preface, [*six*] *petitions, and a conclusion* (*BOC*, WLC 7.288-298).

➢ *The* **PREFACE** *or The Proper Address:*

"Our Father, who art in heaven" (Matthew 6:9a)

Πάτερ ἡμῶν ὁ ἐν τοῖς οὐρανοῖς

Most Christians today are so familiar with the prayer, known by Roman Catholics as the "Our Father" (in Latin, *Pater Noster*), that it may come as a surprise to consider the fact that addressing God as Father was in no way universally accepted in Jesus' day. As we read in the Gospel of John: "For this reason the Jews were seeking all the more to kill (Jesus), because he was not only breaking the sabbath, but was also calling God his own Father, thereby making himself equal to God" (5:18). Nevertheless, John's gospel opens with the assurance that: "to all who received him, who believed in his name, he gave power to become children of God" (John 1:12). There is an important qualification implicit in this statement which is very much worthy of our careful consideration, one that has everything to do with the way in which we relate to our Father in heaven.

Martin Luther wrote, "To this day I suckle at the Lord's Prayer like a child, and as an old man eat and drink from it and never get my fill."[14] Likewise, as Ulrich Luz interprets him, Count Zinzendorf viewed The Lord's Prayer as "the prayer of the born again," for Zinzendorf himself asked: "Dear friends, who can pray like this? Can a person before he or she is born anew from the Holy Spirit, before the divine light of faith has been kindled in his or her soul?"[15]

How then do we reconcile this view, which presupposes Christian faith on the part of the one who prays this prayer, with the popular notion (especially in political circles), so oft repeated, that *every* human being is a child of God? Is it not more accurate to say that every human being is a *creature* of God, but that those who are "born from above" (John 3:1-10), "born of God" (1:13), who receive Christ (1:12), who are themselves a "new creation" (2Cor 5:17; Gal 6:15), are truly "children of God," albeit adopted (Rom 8:23; 9:4; Eph 1:4-6), and co-heirs with Christ (Rom 8:17)?

This is not to approve of judging others, against which presumption we are repeatedly warned (Matt 7:1; Luke 6:37; Rom 2:1; *et al.*), but it is to insist that we exercise spiritual discernment (1John 4:1) and recognize the distinctions which scripture itself makes clear when we develop "eyes to see" and "ears to hear" (cf. Deut 29:4; Mark 4:9, 23; Luke 8:8; 14:35). "Do not judge by appearances, but judge with right judgment" (John 7:24). As unpleasant and disturbing as it is to admit, Jesus himself charged certain of his antagonists, whom we can only assume to be *creatures* of God, with being *children* of "the devil."

> "You are from your father the devil, and you choose to do your father's desires. He was a murderer from the beginning and does not stand in the truth, because there is no truth in him. When he lies, he speaks according to his own nature, for he is a liar and the father of lies" (John 8:44).

What this suggests is *not* that we should, to suit our own purposes, declare who is godly and who is diabolical. It is to suggest, however, that neither pronouncing another a child of the devil nor addressing God as "Our Father" should be done thoughtlessly, hastily, or presumptuously; rather, these cartegories can *only* be rightly employed with due attention to the biblical distinctions between Truth (John 14:6) and falsehood (1John 2:4, 22; 5:10). On the one hand, manifestations of radical evil require that we make spiritual, as well as psychological and physical assessments. In each case, but supremely on spiritual matters, scripture remains the source, basis, and testing ground for our epistemological norms. Christians need not be ashamed of the charge that they entertain "a metaphysical worldview," as though modernity has succeeded in entirely discrediting everything beyond what we can learn from physics, or as though the syncretism of postmodernity could succeed in discrediting not only itself (which it certainly has succeeded in doing time and again), but the biblical revelation of faith and spiritual reality in Christ. On the other hand, God is "our Father" by virtue of *faith*, faith given us by the Holy Spirit, faith which we exercise by receiving Christ (John 1:12-13). God certainly desires that we regard him as "our Father," but our addressing Him as such demands our profound reverence toward Him, as well as our acute wariness of that other father, the "father of lies."

> If you invoke as Father the one who judges all people impartially according to their deeds, live in reverent fear during the time of your exile (1Pet 1:17).
>
> A son honors his father, and servants their master. If then I am a father, where is the honor due me? And if I am a master, where is the respect due me? says the LORD of hosts to you, O priests, who despise my name (Mal 1:6).

Ultimately, Christ Jesus as *the* Son of God has restored to Israel, and has bequeathed to the redeemed of the nations, a stake in the "Father-Son" relationship spoken of by the prophet Isaiah:

> For you are our father,
> though Abraham does not know us
> and Israel does not acknowledge us;
> you, O LORD, are our father;
> our Redeemer from of old is your name (Isa 63:16).

Many more texts could be cited to describe the parental relation between God and Israel, as well as that between God and the Christian believer. In either case, the "adoption to childhood" occurs precisely and even exclusively through Christ and the Holy Spirit (Gal 4:1-9, *et al.*), regardless of whether we read history backwards or forwards. Ultimately the one in whom all things hold together (Col 1:17) is the one who not only teaches this prayer, but also grants us such access that we are able to relate to the Father in this way. As A. J. Worlledge wrote,

> To enter into the real meaning of the teaching of the Sermon on the Mount on prayer, to say in the sense intended by Jesus Christ: 'Our Father, Which art in heaven,' to discern the significance of the great invocation, to exchange anxiety for trustful simplicity of aim, to appropriate in all its power the charter of the efficacy of prayer based on the character of the Father, Who hears His children and knows their needs, is only possible on one condition. The condition lies in the belief that He Who taught us thus to pray is, in truth, One with the Father Whom He revealed, entering into fellowship with men, assuring us in life, in character, in deed and word, that the attributes of God, which had inspired and moulded lives spent in communion with Him, maintained by acts of prayer, are not illusions but realities. It is nothing lower than the fact of the Incarnation of the Son of God which really gives to that sermon as a whole, and not only, though pre-eminently, to its sections on prayer, its lasting influence and power which, had it been merely the utterance of a teacher however great, it could never have possessed, and certainly never retained.[16]

But let us allow the confessional tradition to explain further what we are assuming and what we are saying when we have the courage to address "Our Father, who is in the heavens ..."

❧

I. The Heidelberg Catechism [LORD'S DAY 46]

Q.120. Why has Christ commanded us to address God: "Our Father"?

A. That at the very beginning of our prayer he may awaken in us the childlike reverence and trust toward God which should be the motivation of our prayer, which is that God has become our Father through Christ and will much less deny us what we ask him in faith than our human fathers will refuse us earthly things.

Q.121. Why is there added: "who art in heaven "?

A. That we may have no earthly conception of the heavenly majesty of God, but that we may expect from his almighty power all things that are needed for body and soul (*BOC*, HC 4.120-121).

***II. Westminster Shorter Catechism* (WSC)**

Q.100. What doth the preface of the Lord's Prayer teach us?

A. The preface of the Lord's Prayer, which is, "Our Father which art in heaven," teacheth us to draw near to God with all holy reverence and confidence, as children to a father, able and ready to help us (Isa 64:9; Luke 11:13; Rom 8:15)*; and that we should pray with and for others* (Eph 6:18; Acts 12:5; Zech 8:21) (*BOC*, WSC 7.100).

***III. Westminster Larger Catechism* (WLC)**

Q.189. What doth the preface of the Lord's Prayer teach us?

A. The preface of the Lord's Prayer (*contained in these words, "Our Father which art in heaven"* — Matt 6:9) *teacheth us, when we pray, to draw near to God with confidence of his fatherly goodness, and our interest therein* (Luke 11:13; Rom 8:15)*; with reverence, and all other childlike dispositions* (Ps 95:6-7; Isa 64:9)*, heavenly affections* (Ps 123:1;

Lam 3:41), *and due apprehensions of his sovereign power, majesty, and gracious condescension* (Ps 104:1; Isa 63:15; Ps 113:4-6)*: as also to pray with and for others* (Acts 12:5; Zech 8:21) (*BOC*, WLC 7.299).

1. The First Petition:

"Hallowed be Thy Name" (Matthew 6:9b)

ἁγιασθήτω τὸ ὄνομά σου

These four words, as seemingly simple as they are, are enormously rich and freighted with meaning. Indeed, they are of supreme importance, as they top the list of the six petitions that comprise The Lord's Prayer, and which clearly unfold in a "top down" manner. The hallowing of our heavenly Father's name is to be our highest priority. Yet if this is so, surely this first petition cannot be assumed to exceed in importance, to compete or conflict with what Jesus explicitly states is the "first and greatest commandment," the *shema* of Deuteronomy (6:4-6), that we are to love the Lord our God with all our heart, soul, and mind (Matt 22:37-39). On the contrary, we can only assume that these two supreme statements complement and mutually inform one another. With the commandment to love God ever in view, then, we will clarify the terms in which this first petition is stated, namely, (1) the concept of *hallowing* and the related idea of sanctification; and (2) the particular case of the *holy name of our heavenly Father.* Finally, we will close with some (3) general observations regarding *the name itself.*

i. First, note that *hallow* is simply the verbal form of the adjective *holy.* To render something holy is to hallow it. The Hebrew verb takes various forms of the root word *k-d-sh.* In Greek, the root word is ἁγιάζειν, in Latin, *sanctificare,* from which we derive the English word *sanctify.* But what is holiness? And what "objects" are considered holy, according to scripture? We ask the latter question with caution, however, using the word "object" to refer to the grammatical direct object, rather than to physical objects or artifacts, since the hallowing of objects is the exception rather than the rule in the Old Testament. Some objects are to be hallowed according to the command of the LORD, but beyond these very few and specific items, the hallowing of objects can easily, and often does, come under the category of idolatry.

But what is holiness? Holiness is described in various terms so as to distinguish (1) the pure from the impure (Exod 28:36; 30:35) and (2) the special from the ordinary (Rom 9:21; 2Tim 2:20). The concept of *holiness* occurs widely in scripture.[17] Nevertheless, three particular passages stand out in the Old Testament so as to define the critical distinction between the holy and the unholy. The first occurs at the institution of the Levitical priesthood, in which we read:

> And the LORD spoke to Aaron: Drink no wine or strong drink, neither you nor your sons, when you enter the tent of meeting, that you may not die; it is a statute forever throughout your generations. *You are to distinguish between the holy and the common,*

> *and between the unclean and the clean*; and you are to teach the people of Israel all the statutes that the LORD has spoken to them through Moses (Lev 10:8-11).

The second passage records how the word of the LORD commanded the prophet Ezekiel to say to Israel that they are unclean, due to the fact that the princes (Ezek 22:25), the priests (v. 26), the officials (v. 27) and the prophets (v. 28) have failed to live up to their responsibility and have allowed the people to practice extortion, robbery, and oppression of the poor (v. 29). But it is the priests in particular who have failed with regard to holiness:

> Its priests have done violence to my teaching and have profaned my holy things; they have made no *distinction between the holy and the common*, neither have they taught *the difference between the unclean and the clean*, and they have disregarded my sabbaths, so that I am profaned among them (Ezek 22:26).

Thus, the LORD laments:

> And I sought for anyone among them who would repair the wall and stand in the breach before me on behalf of the land, so that I would not destroy it; but I found no one. Therefore I have poured out my indignation upon them; I have consumed them with the fire of my wrath; I have returned their conduct upon their heads, says the LORD God (Ezek 22:30-31).

The third passage occurs in Ezekiel's promising eschatological vision of the new temple (Ezek 40—48) and its priesthood. There an orthodox remnant of the Levitical priesthood, namely, "the descendants of Zadok, who kept the charge of my sanctuary when the people of Israel went astray from me," says the LORD (44:15), will be those who "shall teach my people *the difference between the holy and the common*, and show them how *to distinguish between the unclean and the clean*" (44:23).

Already we see that holiness is applied to various things. These include *teachings*, *holy things*, and *temporal observances* (22:28). *Temporal observances* include the Sabbath (Gen 2:3; Ezek 20:20); the holy convocations and festivals (Lev 23); the days of the nazirites (Num 6:8); other holidays (Esth 8:17; 9:19, 22); and the (fiftieth) year of Jubilee or "liberty" (Lev 25:10; Isa 61:1-2; Luke 4:16-19). *Holy things* would describe the furnishings of the tabernacle and later the temple, a short list of which is found among those items given into the charge of a clan of the Levites known as the Kohathites: "Their responsibility was to be the ark, the table, the lampstand, the altars, the vessels of the sanctuary with which the priests minister, and the screen — all the service pertaining to these" (Num 3:31). It is worth noting, however, that although the Kohathites were given charge of these holy things, they were commanded "not (to) go in to look on the holy things even for a moment; otherwise they (would) die" (4:20). Other holy things would include the *priestly vestments* (Exod 31:10; 35:19; Lev 16:4, 32; Ezek 42:14); "the *food* by which atonement is made" (Exod 29:33); "all *tithes* from the land" (27:30); the *firstborn* of cow, sheep, and goat (18:17); "the bread of the Presence" or the *showbread* (1Sam 21:4-6).

Finally, with respect to *teachings*, we know that "the law is holy, and the commandment is holy and just and good" (Rom 7:12).

Certain *spaces and places* are also said to be holy, including the ground on which Moses stood when he met the LORD in the burning bush (Exod 3:5; Acts 7:33); the tabernacle (Exod 40:9); Mount Sinai (Exod 19:23); Mount Zion (Ps 87:1; Joel 3:17); the mount of transfiguration (2Pet 1:18); the land to be allotted to the Zadokites and the Levites (Ezek 48:8-14); the city of Jerusalem (Neh 11:1; Isa 52:1); the temple (Ps 5:7; 11:4; 65:4; 79:1; 138:2; Hab 2:20), and preeminently the Holy of Holies (Heb 9:3). Further, the holiness of things has a way of being communicated to places, for as Solomon resolved upon taking the daughter of Pharaoh as his wife: "My wife shall not live in the house of King David of Israel, for the places to which the ark of the LORD has come are holy" (2Chron 8:11).

People are also set aside as holy, including the congregation of Israel itself (Num 16:3); and "the priests and ministering Levites" (2Chron 23:6; Ezra 8:28). In the New Testament, the church is "a chosen race, a royal priesthood, a holy nation, God's own people, in order that you may proclaim the mighty acts of him who called you out of darkness into his marvelous light" (1Pet 2:9). Here too the communicable nature of holiness is such that holiness can be passed from persons to things (Exod 29:22-24), from persons to animals (Lev 8:22-29), and from person to person, as when the Holy Spirit is imparted to someone through the anointing with oil (1Sam 16:13) or the imposition of hands (Acts 8:17; 19:16; *et al.*). Where Timothy's communicable *charism* is concerned — "the gift that is in you, which was given you through prophecy" (1Tim 4:14; cf. Heb 6:2) — Paul describes primarily in terms of the need to teach pure doctrine. None of this is to neglect, however, the simultaneously straightforward and indirect communication, the proclamation of God's mighty acts (1Pet 2:9) unto *faith*, for faith *itself* is holy: the receipt of holy doctrine with the gift of the Holy Spirit; indeed, "faith comes from what is heard, and what is heard comes through the word of Christ" (Rom 10:17).

While in the New Testament certain seemingly obvious physical distinctions begin to be blurred between things, places, and people, e.g., there is no longer Jew or Greek, etc. (Gal 3:28), it is vital to note the distinction between the holy and the common does not! For instance, in the New Testament, people of faith are said to be: the holy temple (1Cor 3:16-17); a spiritual house made of living stones (1Pet 2:4-5); a holy batch of dough and an olive tree that is holy in root and branch (Rom 11:16-24); the body of Christ (1Cor 12:27; Eph 4:11-13), which abides in and is connected to the True Vine (John 15:1-11).

Ultimately, every attribution of holiness to a creaturely form, be it animate or inanimate, is possible only because God alone is holy (1Sam 2:2; Ps 22:3; 1Pet 1:15; Rev 15:4), that is, holy in such a way that all people and things, all times and places, all teachings that are deemed holy derive their holiness strictly and solely from him. We can affirm this by attending to the fact that there are degrees of holiness, i.e. certain things and places are said to be "most holy" (the phrase occurs 46 times in the NRSV). Jesus himself bids us to follow his logic to the source of underived holiness, when he rebukes the religious authorities:

> "Woe to you, blind guides, who say, 'Whoever swears by the sanctuary is bound by nothing, but whoever swears by the gold of the sanctuary is bound by the oath.' You blind fools! For which is

> greater, the gold or the sanctuary that has made the gold sacred? And you say, 'Whoever swears by the altar is bound by nothing, but whoever swears by the gift that is on the altar is bound by the oath.' How blind you are! For which is greater, the gift or the altar that makes the gift sacred? So whoever swears by the altar, swears by it and by everything on it; and whoever swears by the sanctuary, swears by it and by the one who dwells in it; and whoever swears by heaven, swears by the throne of God and by the one who is seated upon it" (Matt 23:16-22).

In other words, all holiness is imparted by none other than the Holy One who has commanded that it be said of himself: "Hear, O Israel: The Lord is our GOD, the Lord alone. You shall love the LORD your God with all your heart, and with all your soul, and with all your might" (Deut 6:4-6). So the greatest commandment also declares that the holy LORD alone is one. The same Jesus who upheld this as the first and greatest commandment also gave us "hallowed be thy name" as the first petition of The Lord's Prayer.

But scripture not only testifies to the fact that Jesus taught us to understand God as the sole source of underived holiness from which all temporal manifestations of holiness derive, it also speaks of Jesus himself as "the Holy One" (Mark 1:24; Luke 4:34; John 6:69; Rev 3:7) who did not experience corruption (Acts 2:27; 13:35; Ps 16:9-10). This is very important to bear in mind so that we do not pit Jesus' teaching over against his atoning work, his unique personhood, or his dual (fully divine and fully human) nature. For our purposes, this means we must not make the mistake of thinking his way of *crossing* the boundaries between holy and unholy (e.g. eating with sinners, touching lepers, etc.) did away with the distinction altogether. This is simply not so, as the first petition itself attests, whereby Jesus teaches us to pray that our heavenly Father's own name be hallowed! Why would such a petition figure as of first importance if the categories of holy and common, clean and unclean, were considered obsolete? On the contrary, rather than doing away with such categories altogether, what Jesus does is unleash God's holiness upon that which is common. Again, though he touched the unclean, he himself did not experience corruption; though he was tested as we are, yet he remained without sin (Heb 4:15); though he was made "to be sin ... so that we might become the righteousness of God," yet he himself "knew no sin" (2Cor 5:21). Where the tearing of the temple veil at his death (Matt 27:51; par) is sometimes mistakenly regarded as the destruction of the distinction between holy and unholy, in fact, this simply means that God's holiness is no longer contained, but is on the loose, waging war against every cause of sin and stumbling in this world.

Much more could be said regarding the concept of holiness, but let it suffice to say that (1) it is not an obsolete category, but one that has been, must be, and will be observed and taught in every generation; (2) it is of paramount importance as it figures in the first petition of The Lord's Prayer; and (3) its one and only source is the same Lord GOD whom we are, as a matter of first importance, to love with all our heart, soul, strength and mind. Thus, there is no disagreement between the first petition and the first commandment.

ii. As with the concept of holiness, the nature of *names*—their inherent meaning, power, and implications—all of these constitute a subject far too vast to treat with any thoroughness here, as does the wonderful variety of the names of God revealed in both Old and New Testaments. Within our present constraints, we will, however, survey the ways in which holiness is attributed to the name of the LORD in scripture, and in this way, gain a better understanding of what is at stake when we pray, "*hallowed be thy name.*" We will limit our scope further, by focussing our attention on the phrase "holy name" as it occurs in the NRSV.

The largest clusters of passages which refer to God's "holy name" occur in *Leviticus, 1Chronicles, Psalms,* and *Ezekiel,* with single occurrences in *Isaiah* and *Amos.* If we address the pertinent texts in canonical order, what is most interesting is how extremely practical are the passages that pertain to the earliest part of Israel's history. Again, there is nothing obsolete about them.

(a) In *Leviticus*, for instance, there is nothing esoteric about the holy name; rather, the LORD is simply and understandably concerned with his reputation — but for the sake of human salvation. That the good LORD'S good name not be associated with evil deeds is of supreme importance. Specifically, the LORD will not tolerate his holy name being associated with crimes which even today threaten to undermine the credibility of the people of faith, namely, child abuse, financial mismanagement of tithes given in sacred trust (dishonest stewards of offerings), and cheating with respect to the quality of acceptable offerings (dishonest givers of offerings). In the first instance, child sacrifice is severely proscribed and carries a capital sentence.

> The LORD spoke to Moses, saying: Say further to the people of Israel: Any of the people of Israel, or of the aliens who reside in Israel, who give any of their offspring to Molech shall be put to death; the people of the land shall stone them to death. I myself will set my face against them, and will cut them off from the people, because they have given of their offspring to Molech, defiling my sanctuary and profaning my holy name. And if the people of the land should ever close their eyes to them, when they give of their offspring to Molech, and do not put them to death, I myself will set my face against them and against their family, and will cut them off from among their people, them and all who follow them in prostituting themselves to Molech (Lev 20:1-5).

This is an admittedly severe sentence, but several references to the cult of the pagan god Molech taken together would suggest that the ritual abuse of children in this cult likely included sexual abuse (Lev 18:21) and sacrificing the children as burnt offerings (2Kings 17:31; 23:10; Jer 32:35; *et al.*). It is possible that this practice "may be of Phoenician origin," though "Deuteronomy explains it as the custom of the indigenous population of Canaan."[18] Without speaking in ethnic, but strictly in spiritual terms, or in terms of spiritual principalities, even the reformer Josiah "did not entirely eradicate" this wicked practice from among the Israelites.[19] Indeed, it is disturbing to realize that the tactic of suicide/homicide bombings continues to claim the lives of children, who are in turn often lauded by their parents as martyrs, in the same general region as Phoenicia, whence the Canaanite and Philistine "sea peoples" and the Caphtorim originated (Gen 10:14; 1Chron 1:12). But the holy name of the LORD will not be associated with such wickedness. On the contrary, Jesus says, in defense of children, "If any of you put a stumbling block before one of these little ones who believe in me, it would be better for you if a great millstone were hung around your neck and you were thrown into the sea" (Mark 9:42).

Likewise, neither the priestly receiver or steward of offerings (Lev 22:2) nor the one who would render offerings acceptable to God (22:32) will be allowed to deal dishonestly with the LORD and thus sully the holy name. It is notable that holiness and sanctity are always characterized by truth (John 17:17-19), while "differing weights are an abomination to the LORD, and false scales are not good" (Prov 20:23). Thus, we see that in Leviticus, the holiness of the name of the LORD pertains to God's strict prohibition of child abuse, and to God's truthful and honest dealings with his people. God's holy name will not be associated with anything false, unjust, abominable, or cruel. Those who accuse the LORD of such things or turn from him on account of them are completely unjustified in doing so.

(b) Three references to the "holy name" in *1Chronicles* all function doxologically. The first two arise with the installation of the ark upon its return to Jerusalem and its installation in the tent David pitched for it. "Glory in his holy name; let the hearts of those who seek the LORD rejoice" (1Chron 16:10). "Save us, O God of our salvation, and gather and rescue us from among the nations, that we may give thanks to your holy name, and glory in your praise" (16:35). A third occasion is also found on the lips of David, who, though he was not allowed to build the temple of the LORD, was allowed to receive the freewill offerings of the people for its construction and gave glory to God for the abundant provisions: "O LORD our God, all this abundance that we have provided for building you a house for your holy name comes from your hand and is all your own" (1Chron 29:16) Thus, in the largely historical book of 1Chronicles, the "holy name" is mentioned strictly with a doxological, even a liturgical purpose. This is somewhat surprising, for while liturgical doxology is what we would expect to find in the cluster that follows, namely, in the Psalter, such consistent doxology is not what the modern reader tends to expect to find in an otherwise largely historical book.

(c) The Psalms contain seven references to the "holy name." Oddly enough, the first occurs in Psalm 30, which bears the anachronistic superscription: "A Song at the dedication of the temple. Of David." While some view this superscription as quite late, pertaining to the cleansing of the temple by Judas Maccabeus (164 BC) and thus to the Festival of Dedication (Hanukkah), it may also pertain to the dedication of the first temple in the Solomonic era. At the very earliest, if David himself were to have had anything to do with its composition, it would have had to have been penned in anticipation of the temple's construction and dedication. Such a view is not inconceivable, since 1Chronicles clearly shows that David was conscious of the fact that he would leave to Solomon the task of constructing and dedicating the temple. As in 1Chronicles, the references to God's "holy name" in the Psalms all function *doxologically*, and grammatically speaking, always as the direct object. But by attending to the particular verbs used and to the parallel

constructions in which the phrase occurs, we may be able to broaden our understanding. Note, for instance, that three times we are urged to "*give thanks* to his (or your) holy name" (Pss 30:4; 97:12; 106:47), which would imply that thanking the holy name is tantamount to thanking God Himself. In these three cases, the verb receives some elaboration by being paired (respectively) with admonitions to "*sing praises to* the LORD" (Ps 30:4) and "*rejoice in* the LORD" (97:12), as well as with the petition that the LORD would save and gather us with the nations, that we may "*glory in* (his) praise" (106:47). Elsewhere, we learn that when we "*trust in* his holy name," such trust is the reason and basis for our gladness of heart (Ps 33:21). Further, there is precedent for our glorying in his praise (Ps 106:7) in the previous psalm, which would suggest again a strong identification between the name, the praise of the name, and the Holy and Glorious One Himself: "*Glory in* his holy name; let the hearts of those who seek the LORD *rejoice*" (Ps 105:3). Again, the LORD himself and his holy name are strongly identified in the most widely known of the Psalms under consideration, which includes the admonition to the finite, human soul to *bless* the LORD, the radical implication of which is that the human soul is actually capable of blessing the Holy One "from whom all blessings flow." "Bless the LORD, O my soul, and all that is within me, bless his holy name" (Ps 103:1). Finally, the laudate psalm juxtaposes the individual's resolution with an amazing eschatological statement: "My mouth will speak the praise of the LORD, and all flesh will bless his holy name forever and ever" (Ps 145:21). What makes these blessings in the psalms directed from humans to the LORD so very remarkable is the fact that they do not seem to square with the proper order of things as they are described in Heb 7:7. "It is beyond dispute that the inferior is blessed by the superior." This is by no means to suggest that the human is ever superior to God, but it is to say that, even in the Psalms, we have a profound demonstration of God's great willingness to undergo an enormous condescension, so as to receive blessings from his human subjects, a condescension closely akin to that described in the Christ hymn of Philippians 2:5-8. In sum, the holy name is to be *praised in song, blessed, thanked, trusted,* not least for the LORD's great condescension. Truly, it is no small thing to bless the LORD! We are to *glory* and *rejoice in* the name, which so completely conveys the presence of God that as we relate to the name in these worshipful ways, we are likewise relating worshipfully to the Holy One Himself. In doing so, we have good reason for *gladness.*

(d) It is in perhaps the least well-known of the major prophets that we find the largest cluster of references to God's "holy name." In Ezekiel we find nine occurrences in eight verses, though these verses are found in only four chapters (20, 36, 39, and 43). As is characteristic of Ezekiel, these passages are highly critical of the nation of Israel, frequently charging the covenant people with profaning the LORD's holy name, and directly attributing their miserable plight in exile to this profanation. In the first reference, the indignation of the LORD is such that he issues an ultimatum, (ironically) placing the first and second commandments at stake—a turning of the divine cheek (Matt 5:39)—and stating that he is prepared to wash his hands of Israel altogether, all for the sake of vindicating his holy name: "As for you, O house of Israel, thus says the Lord GOD: Go serve your idols, everyone of you now and hereafter, if you will not listen to me; but my holy name you shall no more profane with your gifts and your idols" (Ezek 20:39). Nevertheless, the passage is not entirely negative, as it is nested at the heart of a prophesy of restoration (20:33-44).

Likewise, a chapter devoted to the blessing and renewal of Israel contains four consecutive verses, each referring to the "holy name" or to God's sanctifying of his "great name," that which Israel has profaned, that for which the LORD was concerned, and that for the sake of which God resolves to renew Israel, quite despite their idolatries and profanations. In other words, God is again concerned for his reputation, and will act to vindicate his holy name by simultaneously working both for and against Israel, that is, for their purification by giving them a new heart and a new spirit, and by acting against their uncleanness (v. 25), their iniquities, and their abominations (v. 26).

> But when (Israel) came to the nations, wherever they came, *they profaned my holy name*, in that it was said of them, "These are the people of the LORD, and yet they had to go out of his land." But *I had concern for my holy name*, which the house of Israel had profaned among the nations to which they came. Therefore say to the house of Israel, Thus says The Lord GOD: *It is not for your sake, O house of Israel, that I am about to act, but for the sake of my holy name*, which you have profaned among the nations to which you came. I will sanctify my great name, which has been profaned among the nations, and which you have profaned among them; and the nations shall know that I am the LORD, says the Lord GOD, when through you I display my holiness before their eyes (Ezek 36:20-23).

In one of the Bible's most apocalyptic chapters (Ezek 39), the destruction of Gog (vv. 1-20) on the day of the LORD (v. 8) and the regathering of Israel to the land (vv. 21-29) will occasion the LORD's making known his holy name "among (his) people Israel," so as to disallow any future profanation of his holy name, and to identify himself to the Gentiles: "the nations shall know that I am the LORD, the Holy One in Israel" (v. 7). The "fortunes of Jacob" will be restored and mercy shown "to the whole house of Israel." But what is interesting is the LORD's motivation for this decisive, eschatological, restorative act: "I will be jealous (zealous) for my holy name" (v. 25).

Finally, we find two references to the "holy name" in the closing section of Ezekiel, which describes the reconstructed temple. The setting is the prophet's vision of the return of the divine glory [*shekinah*] to the temple.

> He said to me: Son of Man; this is the place of my throne and the place for the soles of my feet, where I will reside among the people of Israel forever. *The house of Israel shall no more defile my holy name*, neither they nor their kings, by their whoring, and by the corpses of their kings at their death. When they placed their threshold by my threshold and their doorposts beside my doorposts, with only a wall between me and them, *they were defiling my holy name* abominations that they committed; therefore I have consumed them in my anger (Ezek 43:7-8).

Again, the hopeful promise in the midst of this convicting rebuke must not be missed. The corpses of the kings will no longer defile, perhaps because this vision concerns life beyond the vision of the valley of dry bones (Ezek 37). It concerns a time when the faithful will live in close proximity to the LORD, even as the kings of old did, as next door neighbors, so to speak, though without defiling the holy name. In the resurrection life, there will be no occasion to bury the bones of former kings.

(e) Two other prophetic passages are worth mentioning. In *Amos*, again the reputation of the LORD is at stake, as the abuse of the poor and immoral sexual relations figure among Israel's compounding transgressions — "for three transgressions ... and for four" — transgressions for which the LORD "will not revoke punishment" (2:6):

> they who trample the head of the poor into the dust of the earth,
> and push the afflicted out of the way;
> father and son go in to the same girl,
> so that my holy name is profaned (2:7).

The second passage, in *Isaiah*, is especially important for two reasons: (1) the fact that it clearly establishes, again by way of a synonymous parallel association, the *eternal* nature of the LORD's holy name; and (2) the fact that the LORD's transcendence, that is, his dwelling in a high, holy, and lofty place, does *not* preclude his simultaneous immanence, his dwelling with the humble and lowly, with those who are contrite in spirit.

> For thus says the high and lofty one
> *who inhabits eternity, whose name is Holy*:
> I dwell in the high and holy place,
> *and also* with those who are contrite

and humble in spirit,
to revive the spirit of the humble,
and to revive the heart of the contrite (Isa 57:15).

Who but the Holy One, who but the LORD can be in two places at once, indeed, can be in any number of places at once, in as many places as there are contrite spirits, and further in such infinitely qualitatively different places as heaven and earth? "For God all things are possible" (Matt 19:26; Mark 10:27; cf. 14:36). Looking forward to the New Testament, then, and even to the new Jerusalem where "there will be no more night," where "they need no light of lamp or sun, for the Lord God will be their light" (Rev 22:5), that is, even as we await the coming, yet future fulfillment of these wondrous promises, we can nevertheless place our full confidence in the present implication, the immanent reality of the promise of Jesus, who said in his farewell discourse, "Those who love me will keep my word, and my Father will love them, and we will come to them and make our home with them" (John 14:23).

iii. So far we have confined our attention to the phrase "holy name" as it occurs in scripture. We have not, however, spoken of the use of the holy name itself, which of course occurs through scripture, especially in the form of the *tetragrammaton*, that is, the four letter Hebrew name which corresponds to the English consonants YHWH, and which is variously translated I AM, or I AM WHO I AM (Exod 3:14). The English reader will recognize the presence of this name by the rendering of the word "LORD," or sometimes "Lord GOD," in small capital letters. The study of the name, the tradition of secrecy surrounding its proper pronunciation, the history of its misinterpretation, would take us beyond the scope of this study. Four points, however, are worth noting.

First, there is the tradition that prohibits the speaking of the name by anyone but the high priest, and then only on the Day of Atonement, and then only in the Holy of Holies. This tradition is reflected in the substitution of the word *Adonai* (Lord or Master) in the Greek translation in the Old Testament, the Septuagint (LXX); and in modern Judaic scholarship (when written or translated in English) by the use of the word G-d, which serves to remind the reader of the holiness of the name and the prohibition against pronouncing it. While we certainly do well to guard against twisting the holy name of God into a warrant for an elitist form of mysticism, on the other hand, a healthy dose of mystery and reverent awe toward the name is quite appropriate and should remind us not to presume too much familiarity with that which is holy, not to "make wrongful use of the name of the LORD your God" (Exod 20:9).

Second, at this point we can see how the third commandment, namely, the negative proscription against the vain use of the name of the LORD (1) is stated positively in the first petition of The Lord's Prayer (thus, you shall not only not misuse the holy name), but you shall actively pray that the name be hallowed, and (2) finds in the light of the first petition its essential unity with the fourth commandment, the positive admonition to hallow the Sabbath, a unity that is discovered in the fact that the petition is taught by the Son of Man, the "Lord of the Sabbath" himself (Matt 12:8).

Third, while the holy name of the LORD and his fatherly relation toward us must remain distinguished from one another, nevertheless, this element of secrecy surrounding the name should remind us of the same discrete ethos which we have considered above concerning our need to address God in secrecy and the intimate use of our personal address to God "our Father in heaven."

Fourth, from a Christian perspective, we do well to remember that Jesus himself has been given the name "above every name."

> Therefore God also highly exalted him
> and gave him the name
> that is above every name,
> so that at the name of Jesus
> every knee should bend,
> in heaven and on earth and under the earth (Phil 2:9-10).

This superlative claim regarding the name of Jesus is neither meant to confuse the Son with the Father, nor to confuse their equally exalted names. Neither does the exaltation of the name of the Son compete with or contradict the exalted name of the Father. On the contrary:

> The Father loves the Son and has placed all things in his hands (John 3:35).
>
> The Father loves the Son and shows him all that he himself is doing; and he will show him greater works than these, so that you will be astonished (John 5:20).
>
> Everyone who believes that Jesus is the Christ has been born of God, and everyone who loves the parent loves the child (1John 5:1)

There is no conflict, but only harmony, between God our Father and God the Son. They both seek the hallowing of the divine name. Neither is there any warrant or any room for polytheistic interpretation. Further, without slipping into modalism, we can say that the name of the Son serves a somewhat different function with respect to prayer, namely, that we are to use it to, in a sense, seal our petitions "in Jesus' name" (John 14:13; 16:26) to ensure that they are consistent and harmonious with the united will and purpose of God the Father and God the Son. But we must consider the "will of God" in conjunction with the third petition.

In light of all the foregoing considerations, it should be clear that we do not take our avoidance of misusing the divine name to the point of hyper-scrupulousness, that is, to the extent that we fail to rightly call upon God as instructed and encouraged. If we err in one direction or the other, we should bear in mind the gracious nature of holy God whom we invoke, allowing Hezekiah's prayer regarding an irregular Passover observance and God's gracious response to it (2Chron 30:18-20) embolden us to more, not less prayer.

This will have to suffice by way of our consideration of the first petition, but before we move on to the second, let us honor our fathers and mothers by considering how they understood this petition, in order to gain further clarity, and hopefully confirm many of our own discoveries.

I. The Heidelberg Catechism (HC) [LORD'S DAY 47]

Q.122. What is the first petition?

A. "Hallowed be thy name." That is: help us first of all to know thee rightly, and to hallow, glorify, and praise thee in all thy works through which there shine thine almighty power, wisdom, goodness, righteousness, mercy, and truth. And so order our whole life in thought, word, and deed that thy name may never be blasphemed on our account, but may always be honored and praised (*BOC*, HC 4.122)

II. Westminster Shorter Catechism (WSC)

Q.101. What do we pray for in the first petition?

A. In the first petition, which is, "Hallowed be thy name," we pray that God would enable us, and others, to glorify him in all that whereby he maketh himself known (Ps 67:1-13; 145; 2Thess 3:1), *and that he would dispose all things to his own glory* (Isa 64:1-2; Rom 11:36) (*BOC*, WSC 7.101).

ߊ

***III. Westminster Larger Catechism* (WLC)**

Q.190. What do we pray for in the first petition?

A. In the first petition (which is, "Hallowed be thy name") (Matt 6:9), *acknowledging the utter inability and indisposition that is in ourselves and all men to honor God aright* (2Cor 3:5; Ps 51:15), *we pray: that God would by his grace enable and incline us and others to know, to acknowledge, and highly esteem him* (Ps 67:2-3; 72:19; Eph 3:20-21), *his titles* (Ps 83:18), *attributes* (Ps 86:10-15; 145:6-8), *ordinances, word* (2Thess 3:1; Ps 107:32; 2Cor 2:14), *works, and whatsoever he is pleased to make himself known by* (Pss 8; 145); *and to glorify him in thought, word* (Ps 19:14), *and deed* (Phil 1:11); *that he would prevent and remove atheism* (Ps 67:1-4; 79:10), *ignorance* (Eph 1:17-18), *idolatry* (Ps 97:7), *profaneness* (Ps 74:18, 22), *and whatsoever is dishonorable to him* (Jer 14:21; 2Kings 19:16); *and by his overruling providence, direct and dispose of all things to his own glory* (Isa 64:1-2; 2Chron 20:6, 10-12) (*BOC*, WSC 7.300).

2. The Second Petition:

"Thy Kingdom come" (Matthew 6:10a)

ἐλθέτω ἡ βασιλεία σου

We have already said that the second petition, "thy kingdom come," is the focus of the eschatological hopes expressed in The Lord's Prayer. This becomes clearer still when we recognize that the final phrase of the verse (6:10c) pertains to the second petition, as well as to the third (6:10b), which separates it from the former (6:10a). In other words, the full version of the second petition should read: "thy kingdom come ... on earth as in heaven." English readers should note that the words "it is," which occur in the third petition: "thy will be done on earth as *it is* in heaven" are supplied in translation only. No equivalent of these words appears in the Greek. Plainly, the second petition asks our heavenly Father to extend his reign, which already governs heaven, to include the earth. Thus we not only await the coming kingdom of our Lord Jesus Christ, we also seek to hasten its coming each time we offer

The Lord's Prayer. But let us organize our considerations according to the profound tension that exists in eschatological thought, the tension between what theologians often abbreviate in terms of the "already" and the "not yet."

i. Already here, but not yet everywhere. A quick glance at the structure of the Gospel of Matthew will remind us that, in the opening chapters when John the Baptist and Jesus came preaching, they were already proclaming: "Repent, for the kingdom of heaven has come near" (3:2; 4:17; cf. 4:23). We do not differentiate between what Matthew normally terms the *kingdom of heaven* and what the other gospel writers call the *kingdom of God*. Simply put, God is already the King of Heaven, and again, our petition calls upon God to extend his heavenly reign to the earth. Nevertheless, it does appear that the kingdom is already close "at hand" long before the Sermon on the Mount begins. So why should we pray for it to come if it is already here? A proper answer requires that we clarify what we mean by *here*.

In fact, the kingdom of heaven is not already established everywhere on earth, but only where *the sovereignty of God* is sought, recognized, welcomed, and obeyed. God is not coercive, but elects, labors for, and offers freedom to human beings (Gal 5:1), while continually hoping humans will come to freely desire God's benevolent sovereignty. Clearly the state of the world today presents countless examples of people and policies, nations and families, which neither seek, perceive, desire, nor adhere to the commandments of God. On the other hand, for those with eyes to see and ears to hear, there are also countless inspiring manifestations of the kingdom of heaven breaking in to our consciousness, and breaking out in the world around us, showing up in startlingly close proximity. It was these manifestations that Jesus would frequently uphold in his parabolic teachings, saying, "The kingdom of heaven is like ..." (Matt 13:31, 33, 44, 45, 47, 52; 20:1). It is also the *nearness* of the kingdom that Jesus indicated to that wise and guileless scribe, who agreed with Jesus in affirming the Great Commandment, and whom Jesus commended by saying, "You are not far from the kingdom of God" (Mark 12:34). Thus we can be comforted by the knowledge that when we pray *"thy kingdom come,"* we are in a very real sense inviting God's sovereignty to extend over us. We are asking God to govern and provide for us as a good King governs and provides for his loyal subjects.

Yet how amazing it is to combine this thought with the fact that our prayer continues to be addressed to Our Father! In other words, the implication of this particular mix of metaphors, taught us by none other than the Son of God himself, is that Our Father is the King of Heaven, and we are the (adopted) children of this King! Clearly we have a major stake in this kingdom and its extension over earthly affairs!

Paul was well aware of this fact when he recorded the words of an early Christian saying: "if we endure, *we will also reign with him*; if we deny him, he will also deny us" (2Tim 2:12; cf. 1Cor 6:3). Likewise, John's eschatological vision records how they are "blessed and holy ... who share in the first resurrection," for over them "the second death has no power, but they will be priests of God and of Christ, and they will reign with him a thousand years" (Rev 20:6). Further, in a passage we earlier considered in light of the first petition, we know that in the new Jerusalem, the saints will "need no light of lamp or sun, for the Lord God will be their light, and *they will reign forever and ever*" (22:5).

Nevertheless, as glorious and promising as all this is, the "already" is obviously not yet "already everywhere." The Great Commission is still in effect (Matt 28:16-20). The scribe whom Jesus commended was deemed "not far" from the kingdom, but he had not yet fully entered it! Put another way, since we are praying for the kingdom to come, not for our being transported to the kingdom, we might say that the "leading edge" of the kingdom has arrived and is particularly evident where the children of God already live according to Christ's teachings. Yet certain parts of the earth still remain in spiritual darkness. Thus the kingdom is still arriving, though certain parts of the world and human society are particularly resistant to it. The Christian does well to remember that heaven is not yet already everywhere; neither it is simply latent on earth. The church in temporality is not yet the church triumphant, but the church militant or (as we say today) the missional church. The kingdom, like the king, arrives from elsewhere, in a certain sense subverting the present order. At the return of "the seventy" who were sent out to preach "the kingdom of God has come near you" (Luke 10:1-12), Jesus told them:

> "I watched Satan fall from heaven like a flash of lightning. See, I have given you authority to tread on snakes and scorpions, and over all the power of the enemy; and nothing will hurt you. Nevertheless, do not rejoice at this, that the spirits submit to you, but rejoice that your names are written in heaven" (Luke 10:18-20).

Indeed, in the Gospel of John, Satan is mentioned as "the ruler of this world" (John 12:31; 14:30; 16:11), and in Ephesians, Paul refers to him as "the ruler of the power of the air, the spirit that is now at work among those who are disobedient" (Eph 2:2). In the synoptic gospels, the demons and the unclean spirits actually recognize Jesus before others do. They identify him as "the Son of God" (Mark 3:1) and "the Holy One of God" (Mark 1:24; Luke 4:34). They are powerless to resist his authority and are terrified at his presence. Indeed, his authority over them gives every indication that Satan's house is divided against itself, that "his end has come" (Mark 3:22-30). This should not be too surprising, since it is characteristic of evil to tend toward disintegration, while by contrast "The LORD is one" (Deut 6:4). Meanwhile, this otherwise alarming episode which precipitates Jesus' teaching on the unforgiveable sin — attributing the good work of the Holy Spirit to Satan or Beelzebul — leaves no doubt as to the superior power of the Holy Spirit over the evil one, but it also makes it clear that Satan himself is responsible for the division of his own house, a division that itself seems to be precipitated by holiness, the holiness of the Holy Spirit. For all this, the good is never to be confused with evil. For as Jesus says regarding the ruler of this world: "He has no power over me" (John 14:30). Or as he says to Pilate, "My kingdom is not from this world. If my kingdom were from this world, my followers would be fighting to keep me from being handed over to the Jews. But as it is, my kingdom is not from here" (John 18:36). With this in mind, we must turn to consider further the sense in which the kingdom of heaven has not yet fully arrived, all the while bearing in mind this governing rule: *The benefits of the kingdom of God may appear, but may not be presumed, where our heavenly Father is not acknowledged as Sovereign or where Jesus Christ is not acknowledged as God's Son and our Lord.*

ii. Not yet everywhere, but already wherever Christ is gratefully acknowledged, joyfully honored, humbly obeyed, and lovingly worshiped as Lord and King. Yes, there are people whose conduct, especially as they direct their "worship" (literally: *worth-ship*) toward worthless things — e.g., spending their time, money, and affections on things which do not satisfy (Isa 55:1-2) — sets them at odds with the kingdom of Christ: "Be sure of this, that no fornicator or impure person, or one who is greedy (that is, an idolater), has any inheritance in the kingdom of Christ and of God" (Eph 5:5).

But what precisely is the kingdom of God and how are we to understand it in relation to the present age, to earthly kingdoms, and to the principalities and powers of this world? The ancient kingdoms mentioned in scripture are portrayed in overwhelmingly negative terms. The first kingdom mentioned is Babel (Gen 10:10). The first kings are mentioned in connection with the battle of "four kings against five" (Gen 14:1-9) in which the Kings of Sodom and Gomorrah were initially defeated and Lot captured (14:11-12). After Abram defeats the four conquering kings and rescues Lot, he is met by the grateful King of Sodom, but the outstanding figure in the landscape is the mysterious King Mechizedek of Salem, who brings to Abram bread and wine. He is said to be "priest of God Most High" (14:18), and from a New Testament perspective, this mysterious priestly king is said to be "without father, without mother, without genealogy, having neither beginning of days nor end of life, but resembling the Son of God, he remains a priest forever" (Heb 7:3), and is thus an antetype, a figure of Christ. Melchizedek is the earliest pattern for "the house of Jacob" as Moses is told to address them: "you shall be for me a *priestly kingdom* and a holy nation" (Exod 19:6).

In contrast to the proto-Messianic Melchizedek and to the LORD's intentions for Israel to serve as a priestly kingdom, the kings of scripture are paradigms of corruption: Abimelech king of the Philistines, Sihon king of the Amorites, Og king of Bashon, Agag king of the Amalekites. With such a rogue's gallery representing the kings of the surrounding nations, we can understand the LORD's indignation when Israel says to Samuel, the LORD's prophet: "appoint for us, then, a king to govern us, like other nations" (1Sam 8:5). Samuel, we are told, was "displeased" by this, prayed to the LORD (8:6), and received the following answer: "Listen to the voice of the people in all that they say to you; for they have not rejected you, but *they have rejected me from being king over them*" (8:7).

This event is of utmost importance for understanding the significance of the fact that when Jesus comes preaching, the *content* of his message is *the kingdom of God*. For his doing so represents the vindication of God's governance of Israel and ultimately of the nations after centuries of decline. And what a decline! After the monarchy's false start with King Saul, God's own object lesson of the foolishness of human kings, Kings David and Solomon represent the glory days of the kingdom of Israel. But even their relatively few imperfections are severe and sow the seeds of disobedience, idolatry, corruption, and civil war. The books of 1–2Kings and 1–2Chronicles record the gradual but relentless fragmentation and collapse of the kingdoms of Israel and Judah. This depressing decline is mitigated only occasionally by a few relatively good kings of Judah, like Asa, Hezekiah, and Josiah, who are yet fallible and whose reforms never quite go far enough. After the capture and dispersion of the northern tribes by the king of Assyria, Judah holds out only a little longer and Jerusalem is finally besieged by and falls to the king of Babylon (587 BC). 2Kings concludes with the family of the puppet king Zedekiah being cut down before his eyes, his own eyes being put out, and the legitimate heir, Jehoiachin, in captivity. Yet we we are told of this heir, "every day of his life he dined regularly" in the presence of King Evil-Merodach of Babylon, who (despite his name which seems oddly apt to the English reader) nevertheless treated Jehoiachin kindly (2Kings 27-30; cf. Jer 22:24-30).

The lines of the kings of Israel and Judah become quite murky with the exile, a problem Matthew (1:1-17) and Luke (3:23-38) each seek to address through their genealogies. Some clues to the continuity of the line of kings exist in 1–2Chronicles, Ezra (and in the apocryphal books of Esdras), and elsewhere; but, with the return of the exiles only some seventy years later and certain figures — namely, Ezra, Zerubbabel, and preeminently Joshua (cf. Zech 3:1-9) — working to restore the city wall and the temple, there is, significantly, no more discussion of kings. The post-exilic community is, even through the time of Jesus, consistently under the temporal dominion of some imperial power: Persian, Greek, Seleucid, Roman. No wonder the inscription on the sign hung above Jesus on the cross, reading: "King of the Jews," though true in earnest, was regarded by Jew and Gentile alike as cruelly ironic (John 19:19-22). The mere thought of a Jewish king was patently absurd.

Yet the human ancestry of Jesus' surrogate human father Joseph (Matt 1:16; Luke 3:23) is of only relative importance. Paul even goes so far as to sternly warn against making too much of genealogies (1Tim 1:4; Titus 3:9). For, as we have said, the kingdom of heaven, the reign of Christ Jesus, is not of this world (John 18:36), and this otherworldliness befits his conception by the Holy Spirit (Matt 1:18; Luke 1:34-35) and his status as the only begotten Son and heir of the heavenly Father. Neither do we assume the kingdom of heaven is, fully and finally, already here. One important parable that Jesus told concerning the coming kingdom that is not yet fully come, occurs in Luke's version of the parable of the pounds (Luke 19:11-27), as distinct from Matthew's parable of the talents (Matt 25:14-30). In Luke we are told at the outset that Jesus "went on to tell a parable, because he was near Jerusalem, and because they supposed that the kingdom of God was to appear immediately. So he said, 'A nobleman went to a distant country to get royal power for himself and then return'" (19:11-12). The parable unfolds according to the same pattern we find in Matthew, with one key difference being that the trustworthy stewards of the nobleman's pounds are rewarded with a charge to rule over a number of cities commensurate with their management of the pounds (Luke 19:17, 19). We are also given the sad but arresting detail that "the citizens of his country hated (the nobleman) and sent a delegation after him, saying,

'We do not want this man to rule over us'" (19:14). Further, we have the still more sobering report that, "When he returned, having received royal power" (19:15), he said, "as for these enemies of mine who did not want me to be king over them—bring them here and slaughter them in my presence" (19:27). What all of this indicates is that the coming of the kingdom of Christ: (1) involves his going on a great journey; (2) that his errand involves gaining royal power; and (3) that those who hate him or reject him as their ruler will be dealt with in a far different fashion than those who welcome his reign and manage his assets responsibly, loyally, energetically, and accountably.

Thus Paul would write to Timothy with such tremendous confidence at the end of his life, precisely because he and Timothy *did* long for Christ's appearing:

> *In the presence of God and of Christ Jesus*, who is to judge the living and the dead, and *in view of his appearing and his kingdom*, I solemnly urge you: proclaim the message; be persistent whether the time is favorable or unfavorable; convince, rebuke, and encourage, with the utmost patience in teaching. For the time is coming when people will not put up with sound doctrine, but having itching ears, they will accumulate for themselves teachers to suit their own desires, and will turn away from listening to the truth and wander away to myths. As for you, always be sober, endure suffering, do the work of an evangelist, carry out your ministry fully.
>
> As for me, I am already being poured out as a libation, and the time of my departure has come. I have fought the good fight, I have finished the race, I have kept the faith. From now on there is reserved for me the crown of righteousness, which the Lord, the righteous judge, will give me on that day, and not only to me but also *to all who have longed for his appearing* (2Tim 4:1-8).

Somewhat earlier, Paul closed his first letter to Timothy thus:

> In the presence of God, who gives life to all things, and of Christ Jesus, who in his testimony before Pontius Pilate made the good confession, I charge you to keep the commandment without spot or blame *until the manifestation of our Lord Jesus Christ, which he will bring about at the right time—he who is the blessed and only Sovereign, the King of kings and Lord of lords. It is he alone who has immortality and dwells in unapproachable light, whom no one has ever seen or can see; to him be honor and eternal dominion. Amen.*
>
> *As for those who in the present age* are rich, command them not to be haughty, or to set their hopes on the uncertainty of riches, but rather on God who richly provides us with everything for our enjoyment. They are to do good, to be rich in good works, generous, and ready to share, thus storing up for themselves the treasure of a good foundation for the future, so that they may take hold of the life that really is life (1Tim 6:13-19).

This passage raises an important issue for our understanding Christian discourse regarding "the kingdom." When we speak of *the* kingdom, using the definite article, clearly we are affirming with Paul that God the Father and Christ the Son are one, and simultaneously co-regents of the one kingdom, which in the end is the only kingdom that will endure. It is an expression of our certain hope and our expectant faith in the final victorious outcome: Our God *will* reign on earth.

Meanwhile, Paul also speaks of "the present age" (6:17; Titus 2:12) in contrast to "the age to come," and in a way that reminds us of the co-regency of the Father and the Son and of the supremacy of the hallowed name.

> God put (his) power to work in Christ when he raised him from the dead and seated him at his right hand in the heavenly places, far above all rule and authority and power and dominion, and above every name that is named, *not only in this age but also in the age to come.* And he has put all things under his feet and has made him the head over all things for the church, which is his body, the fullness of him who fills all in all (Eph 1:20-23).

Jesus likewise speaks in terms that contrast the present and the coming ages (Matt 12:32; Mark 10:3; Luke 18:30), the latter pertaining to "eternal life." This contrast between the "two ages" is today frequently considered theologically simplistic or even dismissed as dualistic, but in fact it is an extremely important dialectic that gives rise to a number of vital distinctions:

- the two ways (Ps 1; *Didache* 1): the one wide which leads to destruction and the other narrow which leads to life (Matt 7:13-14);
- the "infinite qualitative difference" between the Spirit of truth (John 14:17; 15:26; 16:13; 1John 4:6) and the lying spirit of antichrist (1John 2:18, 22; 4:3; 2John 7);
- the quantitative temporal distinction between present and future, or between the present form of the world which is passing away (1Cor 7:31; 1John 2:9) and the coming kingdom;
- the "infinite qualitative difference" between time (temporality) and eternity (1John 2:17);
- the "infinite qualitative difference" between earth and heaven: *"God is in heaven, and you upon earth; therefore let your words be few"* (Eccl 5:2).

Theologically, when we speak in such terms, it is important to clearly define what it is we are deliberating. For instance, *epistemology* pertains to how we know what we know, i.e. the difference between truth and error (1John 4:6), or the exercise of spiritual discernment (Matt 7:16-20; Rom 12:2; 1Cor 1:19; 2:14-15; 11:29; 12:10; 1John 4:1); *soteriology* pertains to and impinges upon the distinction between the regenerate and the unregenerate, between salvation and destruction; while *sanctification* pertains to our spiritual maturation under the influence of the Spirit as we live the Christian life on the way (classically speaking) from one kingdom to another.[20]

The second petition of The Lord's Prayer, however, is probably best understood in light of the particular distinctions that occur alongside the prayer in the Sermon on the Mount, especially those which arise later in Matthew 6:

- between treasure in heaven and treasure on earth (6:19-21);
- between "the two masters," that is, the eternal God and temporal mammon (6:24);
- between those who do not worry, but trust in their righteous Sovereign to provide abundantly for his subjects, and the pagans who worry endlessly about tomorrow's temporal needs and thus have no father in God (6:25-34).

A fully developed understanding of the kingdom of God must, as we have said, take sufficient account of Jesus' teaching regarding the kingdom, especially in the parables. Nevertheless, a great deal of scholarship in the last century has tended to focus on the parables with little attention given to the ways in which Christ's kingdom is revealed in his miracles and pre-eminently in his "work" on the cross, which includes, among many other things, his thorny coronation, his words spoken from the cross, and the sense in which the sign placed above his head was simultaneously ironic (indirect) and earnest (direct). In other words, the coming kingdom is one that will not simply be a new and just social order, a commonwealth with no sovereign, a body with no head, as many hyperpolitical interpreters claim who focus solely on the parables, dismiss the miracles, and avoid the cross. But the coming of the kingdom will come with the King whose power and glory will manifestly vindicate all that he and his followers have suffered in the present age.

But let us conclude these deliberations by again allowing our confessional statements to inform, guide, and summarize our thoughts with respect to the second petition.

I. The Heidelberg Catechism (HC) [LORD'S DAY 48]

Q.123. What is the second petition?

A. "Thy kingdom come." That is: so govern us by thy Word and Spirit that we may more and more submit ourselves unto thee. Uphold and increase thy church. Destroy the works of the devil, every power that raises itself against thee, and all wicked schemes thought up against thy holy Word, until the full coming of thy kingdom in which thou shalt be all in all (*BOC*, HC 4.123).

II. Westminster Shorter Catechism **(WSC)**

Q.102. What do we pray for in the second petition?

A. In the second petition, which is, "Thy kingdom come," we pray that Satan's kingdom may be destroyed (Ps 68:1), *and that the Kingdom of grace may be advanced, ourselves and others brought into it, and kept in it* (2Thess 3:1; Ps 51:18; 67:1-3; Rom 10:1), *and that the Kingdom of glory may be hastened* (Rev 22:20; 2Pet 3:11-13) (*BOC*, WSC 7.102).

III. Westminster Larger Catechism **(WLC)**

Q.191. What do we pray for in the second petition?

A. In the second petition (which is, "Thy Kingdom come") (Matt 6:10), *acknowledging ourselves and all mankind to be by nature under the dominion of sin and Satan* (Eph 2:2-3), *we pray: that the kingdom of sin and Satan may be destroyed* (Ps 68:1; Rev 12:9), *the gospel propagated throughout the world* (2Thess 3:1), *the Jews called* (Rom 10:1; Ps 67:2), *the fullness of the Gentiles brought in* (Rom 11:25; Ps 67:1-7); *that the church may be furnished with all gospel-officers and ordinances* (Matt 9:38), *purged from corruption* (Eph 5:26-27; Mal 1:11), *countenanced and maintained by the civil magistrate; that the ordinances of Christ may be purely dispensed, and made effectual to the converting of those that are yet in their sins, and the confirming, comforting,and building up of those that are already converted* (2Cor 4:2; Acts 26:18; 2Thess 2:16-17)*; that Christ would rule in our hearts here* (Eph 3:14, 17)*, and hasten the time of his second coming, and our reigning with him forever* (Rev 22:20)*; and that he would be pleased so to exercise the Kingdom of his power in all the world, as may best conduce to these ends* (Isa 64:1-2; 2Chron 20:6, 10-12) (*BOC*, WLC 7.301).

3. The Third Petition:

"Thy will be done on earth as it is in heaven"

(Matthew 6:10b, c)

γενηθήτω τὸ θέλημά σου
ὡς ἐν οὐρανῷ καὶ ἐπὶ [της] γῆς

The two most interesting words here are the verb γενηθήτω and the noun θέλημά. The verb literally means *to become, to come about, to happen, to arise*. We might say more paraphrastically, *let it take shape* or *materialize*. The noun means one's *wish, will,* or *desire*. The meaning of the petition is simple: "*may your will come about*" or "*may what you desire materialize.*" What is not simple at all is to live with the implications of this petition. Finally, the most important of these words is the genitive (possessive) pronoun *thy* [σου], particularly as it is applied to God. Indeed, it is the third such use of this pronoun, which concludes each of the first three petitions in rhythmic, rhyming fashion. For what we are asking is that God's will, not ours, be done. In Greek, the stress falls on *thine, thine, thine!*

Let us consider this simple petition according to the following outline: (1) the *relative*, but not absolute, *renunciation of the human will* that is implicit in the petition; (2) the question of *what God's will is generally,* that is, in accordance with God's overall redemptive purpose as this is revealed in scripture; and (3) what we can know of *God's specific will* for our lives, be it understood in socio-political, ecclesial, familial, or individual terms.

i. the relative (not absolute) renunciation of the human will

As we petition our heavenly Father, "thy will be done," we are implicitly, but nevertheless obviously, subordinating our human self-will to the divine will. It is important to note, however, that while Jesus prays in the Garden of Gethsemane, "Father, if you are willing, remove this cup from me; yet, not my will but yours be done" (cf. Luke 22:42; cf. Matt 26:41), he still acknowledges that he has a human will. His human will is not abolished, but subordinated or suspended. His renunciation of his will, if we can call it that, is relative, not absolute, even though the cost of this renunciation on this occasion will have absolutely decisive consequences for his own mortal body and, from the perspective of Christian faith, for the salvation of human beings and for the renovation of creation. He assents to the One who sees the complete picture as even Jesus himself cannot see it, that is, the Father whose authority—in certain temporal respects—exceeds that of Jesus, both as the Son of God (John 5:19, 30) and as the Son of Man (Mark 10:40; 13:32).

We should take with equal seriousness both the resolute "*I shall not want*" and the fact that the Shepherd LORD "*makes* me lie down in green pastures." In other words, the things he does *to* me are as important for my well being as the things he does *for* me: "he leads me beside still waters; he restores my soul. He leads me in right paths;" but again, these things he does "for his name's sake" (Ps 23:1-4). That our wants, needs, and desires are not to govern us does not make them disappear. But, as we observed in considering the second petition, we can bring our wants under the sovereign will of God with the assurance that the Shepherd King of the Kingdom will provide for our needs: "your heavenly Father knows that you need all these things. But strive first for the kingdom of God and his righteousness, and all these things will be given to you as well" (Matt 6:32-33).

The idea that praying this petition subordinates the human will to the divine will raises the question of the *freedom of the Christian*, and perhaps even suggests to some that God's will is deterministic, that God does not desire the human to be free. Nothing could be further from the truth. Indeed, Jesus said, "If you continue in my word, you are truly my disciples; and you will know the truth, and the truth will make you free" (John 8:31-32). Clearly God wills our freedom,[21] yet in his wisdom, God knows that the truth, the Truth being Christ, is our way to freedom (John 14:1-6). Paul states quite clearly that God intends and wills the freedom of the Christian: "For freedom Christ has set us free. Stand firm, therefore, and do not submit again to a yoke of slavery" (Gal 5:1). How then are we to understand the admonition to embrace the "light" and "easy" yoke of Christ (Matt 11:29-30) or to be the "slave of all" (Mark 10:43-44)? By recognizing that these, in fact, constititute "continuing in Christ's word," which is not only to be understood in terms of following his teaching, but also in terms of abiding in him apart from whom we can do nothing (John 15:5). Again, he is the Truth and our Way to freedom, and we remain in him by obeying his teachings. In this way, we can say that faith understood as obedience is not *the means* to our freedom; rather, such faith *is* our freedom. We are most free when we pray: "*thy will be done*." Note the startling contrast between spiritual and earthly freedom in the fact that Jesus uttered this petition and was immediately arrested thereafter. Did his arrest make him unfree? Not at all. Rather, he himself "continued in the word," which is the way to freedom (John 8:31), saying, "let the scriptures be fulfilled" (Matt 26:54).

We stand in a tension between temporal bondage and eternal freedom. God's will is sovereign, but God's will is such that God is also more concerned with setting us free than we are, who are prone to return to the wrong kind of slavery. Yet, the sovereignty of God's will is not such that God refuses to consider the will and desire of the human. Jesus says: "Ask ...; seek ...; knock ..." (Luke 11:9), and promises it will be given, found, opened. God desires, respects, and responds to our prayers. God wills and invites, indeed, God *awaits* our participation in the outworking of his will. Thus when we read Job's lament that God does not seem to be acting on his complaint — "But he stands alone and who can dissuade him? What he desires, that he does" (Job 23:13) — we must place this in its proper sphere. Such passages testify to God's ultimate freedom, yet they also need to be taken in light of those occasions where God has in fact allowed his mind to be changed, e.g., at the intercessions of Moses (Exod 32:11-14), and at the repentance of the Ninevites (Jon 3:5-10). This is the sort of tension in which we must try and understand God's will, in which we should recognize God's determination, resolve, and ultimate victory, but not attribute to the sovereignty of God's will any heavy-handedness or any violation of humankind's relative freedom, as we might be tempted to do if we were speaking of an overpowering human will and not the divine will.

The specific circumstances that figure in God's will and take concrete form in our daily existence must be understood in light of God's redemptive purpose. Therefore, let us examine what we can positively state with regard to "God's will" as this phrase is applied to "the divine plan."

ii. God's general will and overall redemptive purpose. We can be assured that we are proceeding correctly in this top down fashion, so to speak, by considering *first* the *telos* or purpose of God's overarching divine plan and only *secondarily* trying to clarify the specifics. If this seems overly bold on our part, it is not in ourselves that we have such boldness, but "this is the boldness we have *in him*, that *if we ask anything according to his will, he hears us*" (1John 5:14). In other words, those things we are to seek, we are also to measure, test, and evaluate "according to his will." There are some things for which we are *not* to pray (1John 5:16), and there are certain motivations that undermine the credibility and sincerity of our petitions (Jas 4:3). But where we honor and seek the fulfillment of God's purpose, God is eager and happy to involve us in his reconciling ministry (2Cor 5:18) and is glorified thereby. But what precisely can we know of our Father's grand scheme?

First, God *wills* the salvation of all: "For I have no pleasure in the death of anyone, says the Lord GOD. Turn, then, and live" (Ezek 18:32). "The Lord is not slow about his promise, as some think of slowness, but is patient with you, not wanting any to perish, but all to come to repentance" (2Pet 3:9). This is especially apparent when we consider that *repentance* and *faith* are, for all practical purposes identical, or at least synonymous (Mark 1:14-15; Rom 14:23).

Second, God's charitable, merciful, and long-suffering will is not only all-encompassing in intent, it is also described in such a way that confirms what we have said above regarding our relation to God as his (adopted) children through faith:

> He destined us for adoption as his children through Jesus Christ, according to the good pleasure of his will, to the praise of his glorious grace that he freely bestowed on us in the Beloved that he lavished on us. With all wisdom and insight he has made known to us the mystery of his will, according to his good pleasure that he set forth in Christ, as a plan for the fullness of time, to gather up all things in him, things in heaven and things on earth (Eph 1:5-10).

Third, that God *wills* the salvation of all, does *not* means that God *guarantees* salvation to those who do not come to faith in Christ. For Christ Jesus is "the guarantee of a better covenant" (Heb 7:22). If we reject the guarantee, we reject the covenant of faith. But, the Holy

Spirit is the gift of faith: "He who has prepared us for this very thing is God, who has given us the Spirit as a guarantee" (2Cor 5:5). Where repentance and faith are identified (i.e., understood as identical and distinguished only by way of the prepositional referent: *from/to*), we can say God wills that all should come to faith (2Pet 3:9). Faith and the Spirit are inseparable. Further, the divine plan, or "*economy*," is revealed precisely to faith: "the divine training [οἰκονομίαν] ... is known by faith" (1Tim 1:3-4). Likewise, it is the Spirit who "searches everything, even the depths of God" (1Cor 2:9-10). Yes, God wills all to come to salvation through faith (Eph 2:8-10), but it still remains within the realm of possibility that some will neglect this great salvation, a concern clearly expressed in the Epistle to the Hebrews:

> Therefore we must pay greater attention to what we have heard, so that we do not drift away from it. For if the message declared through angels was valid, and every transgression or disobedience received a just penalty, how can we escape if we neglect so great a salvation? It was declared at first through the Lord, and it was attested to us by those who heard him, while God added his testimony by signs and wonders and various miracles, and by gifts of the Holy Spirit, distributed according to his will (Heb 2:1-4).

We see God's revelatory method here is in no way manipulative or coercive, but simply emphasizes declaration and testimony; his respect for human freedom is such that he will not violate it, despite the quality of omnipotence popularly (and often simplistically) attributed to him. But God will give the Holy Spirit readily (Luke 11:13) and without measure (John 3:34), so that faith and the Spirit are always available to those in need of salvation. Thus, they are without excuse who never come to faith (Rom 1:20-21).

Fourth, the wide and immeasurable outpouring of God's own Spirit is clearly part of God's will for human salvation through faith:

> Then afterward,
> I will pour out my spirit on all flesh;
> your sons and your daughters shall prophesy,
> your old men shall dream dreams,
> and your young men shall see visions.
> Even on the male and female slaves,
> in those days, I will pour out my spirit.
> I will show portents in the heavens and on the earth, blood and fire and columns of smoke. The sun shall be turned to darkness, and the moon to blood, before the great and terrible day of the Lord comes. Then everyone who calls on the name of the Lord shall be saved; for in Mount Zion and in Jerusalem there shall be those who escape, as the Lord has said, and among the survivors shall be those whom the Lord calls (Joel 2:28-32).

Meanwhile, it is abundantly clear that faith is a gift of the same Spirit (1Cor 12:31–13:13), as is repentance (Acts 5:31; 11:18) with which we must continue to identify faith, specifically, the "obedience of faith" (Rom 1:5; 16:26). So what is known as the *ordo salutis* [the "order" or steps by which we come to salvation] likewise derives from the gift of the Spirit, who gives the gift of faith as one receive and confesses faith in the Word of God, Jesus Christ as Lord and the gospel of his resurrection from the dead (Rom 10:5-17).

Fifth, not only is the Holy Spirit everywhere available to us for salvation, but the angels are also, by definition, "spirits in the divine service, sent to serve for the sake of those who are to inherit salvation" (Heb 1:14; cf. Ps 103:20).

Sixth, God's will is that we should bear witness, not only as a means to the end of making the good news known to all, but as the end in itself. God desires that all should witness his glory for themselves. "No longer shall they teach one another, or say to each other, 'Know the LORD,' for they shall all know me, from the least of them to the greatest, says the LORD; for I will forgive their iniquity, and remember their sin no more" (Jer 31:34).

Seventh, God wills that we should be made complete or perfect so that we may do his will to his good pleasure (Heb 13:20-21): "Be perfect, therefore, as your heavenly Father is perfect" (Matt 5:48).

Eighth, God wants us to partake of, to "taste and see" his goodness (Ps 34:8), and to enjoy his divine nature:

> His divine power has given us everything needed for life and godliness, through the knowledge of him who called us by his own glory and goodness. Thus he has given us, through these things, his precious and very great promises, so that through them you may escape from the corruption that is in the world because of lust, and may become participants of the divine nature (2Pet 1:3-4).

Finally, God has already made marvelous provision for this in his amazing and far-reaching acts of creation and redemption:

> You are worthy, our Lord and God,
> to receive glory and honor and power,
> for you created all things,
> and by your will they existed and were created (Rev 4:11)

> And it is by God's will that we have been sanctified through the offering of the body of Jesus Christ once for all (Heb 10:10).

iii. God's specific and particular will for our (socio-political, ecclesial, familial, and individual) lives. Scripture also testifies to the manner in which we are to seek God's will with regard to our specific circumstances, even as it reminds us that we are to understand the contingency of our circumstances in relation to the will of God. Entrepreneurial endeavors, for example, may be allowed or suspended by God's will:

> Come now, you who say, 'Today or tomorrow we will go to such and such a town and spend a year there, doing business and making money.' Yet you do not even know what tomorrow will bring. What is your life? For you are a mist that appears for a little while and then vanishes. Instead you ought to say, 'If the Lord wishes, we will live and do this or that' (Jas 4:13-15).

Paul was in the practice of submitting his specific travel plans for his missionary journeys for the Lord's approval (Acts 18:21; Rom 1:10; 15:32; 1Cor 4:19; cf. Acts 21:14). At one point, Luke includes this remarkable report: "They went through the region of Phrygia and Galatia, having been forbidden by the Holy Spirit to speak the word in Asia. When they had come opposite Mysia, they attempted to go into Bithynia, but the Spirit of Jesus did not allow them" (Acts 16:6-7).

Elsewhere, the general admonition to good moral conduct is identified as one means by which "you should silence the ignorance of the foolish" (1Pet 2:15), while the specific instance of suffering may arise as an occasion to exercise faith and bear witness to God's faithfulness by maintaining good conduct despite the suffering (1Pet 3:17; 4:19).

The Old Testament records numerous examples in which the particulars of God's will are discerned. Among the most familiar are:

- Gideon's use of a fleece on two occasions to determine if the LORD wanted him to attack the Midianites (Judges 6:37-40);
- The coordination of David's attack on the Philistines with the sound of marching in the trees (2Sam 5:23-24);
- the casting of lots: to identify the scapegoat (Lev 16:8); for the apportionment of the land (Josh 18:10); to identify Jonah as the object of God's anger (Jon 1:7); and to choose a replacement for Judas (Acts 1:26);
- the use of the Urim and Thummim (Num 27:21) by Eleazar the priest under Joshua to inquire regarding the comings and goings of the Israelites.

Nevertheless, we should exercise considerable caution with respect to seeking *methods* (Eph 4:14; 6:11). For, in fact, scripture takes an extremely dim view of the practice of "divination." Acting as a medium or wizard was a capital offence (Lev 20:27). Saul's consultation of the medium or witch of Endor was a rebellion of the worst sort (1Sam 28:7; 1Chron 10:13). Jesus, of course, sighs heavily when the Pharisees ask him for a sign from heaven and he refuses to give them one (Matt 8:11-12). Asking for one, he says, is itself a sign of "an evil generation" (Luke 11:29). In fact, it may well be that what is "evil" about such a request is that it indicates our preference for signs other than the ones God has already given, and thus our rejection of God's self-revelation.

What we can say with certainty is that when *God* initiates a sign, it is a grace to be received with gratitude and with prayers that the Spirit would help us to understand it properly. Such signs would surely include the lamb's blood on the houses at the Exodus by which the Israelites were preserved from the tenth plague (Exod 12:13); the sign of Immanuel (Isa 7:14); and preeminently, the sign heralded by the angels: "This will be a sign for you: you will find a child wrapped in bands of cloth and lying in a manger" (Luke 2:12). These divinely initiated signs, of course, indicate of God's redemptive plan by which we should measure and test, and to which we should seek to conform, our own wills, praying, "I delight to do your will, O my God; your law is within my heart" (Ps 40:8), and "Teach me to do your will, for you are my God. Let your good spirit lead me on a level path" (Ps 143:10).

We can resolve this dilemma between the temptation to ask for signs and our legitimate desire to discern God's specific will for our lives in this way: while an evil generation wants a sign of heaven, those who seek first the kingdom of God and his righteousness want heaven itself, so to speak. More precisely, they desire no one other than the God of heaven himself to extend his reign over all the earth. They long to live in God and abide in Christ by faith, by the gift of the Holy Spirit. For them, repentance and faith is a new realm altogether in which they are to develop new powers of perception, spiritual eyes and ears, to perceive not mere signs of something that is not there, but the real reality of which they are now a part as co-heirs with Christ. Of those who seek and find and live in the kingdom of God, Jesus says: "Blessed are the eyes that see what you see! For I tell you that many prophets and kings desired to see what you see, but did not see it, and to hear what you hear, but did not hear it." (Luke 10:23-24; cf. Matt 13:17). In the kingdom, we are to hear the Word with our ears, by which hearing comes faith itself with the Holy Spirit, comes the kingdom. Perception in the kingdom is not reducible to signs, but is perception by faith, in faith. Neither is the human relation to God to be reduced to or replaced by a mere method for determining God's will. God's mercies are new every morning (Lam 3:22). Thus, those who stand in obedient, worshipful relation to God as Sovereign Father are not to seek some slavish system or predictable interactive program in lieu of God and his merciful and often delightful way of revealing his will, one step at a time, to faith. "We walk by faith, and not by sight" (2Cor 5:6-7).

In this, Christ is the model, "the pioneer and perfecter of our faith" (Heb 12:2). Paul writes: "Let the same mind be in you that was in Christ Jesus" (Phil 2:5); "Do not be conformed to this world, but be transformed by the renewing of your minds, so that you may discern what is the will of God—what is good and acceptable and perfect" (Rom 12:2). It is significant that the word μετάνοια [to *repent*] literally means to *change one's mind.* We can interpret this as urging us to conform to Christ's own thinking, his manner of discerning and acting on God's will. Though he alone is our sacrifice — we are no substitute for him, but he was for us! — yet we *are* his ambassadors, "since God is making his appeal through us" (2Cor 5:20). Therefore, we do well to measure our understanding of God's specific will for us according to the reconciling work of Christ, recognizing that he has abolished sacrifices required by the law in order to establish the will of God.

> Since the law has only a shadow of the good things to come and not the true form of these realities, it can never, by the same sacrifices that are continually offered year after year, make perfect those who approach. ... For it is impossible for the blood of bulls and goats to take away sins. Consequently, when Christ came into the world, he said,
>
> "Sacrifices and offerings you have not desired,
> but a body you have prepared for me;
> in burnt offerings and sin offerings
> you have taken no pleasure.
> Then I said, 'See, God, I have come to do your will, O God'
> (in the scroll of the book it is written of me)."
>
> When he said above, "You have neither desired nor taken pleasure in sacrifices and offerings and burnt offerings and sin offerings" (these are offered according to the law), then he added, "See, I have come to do your will." He abolishes the first in order to establish the second. And it is by God's will that we have been sanctified through the offering of the body of Jesus Christ once for all (Heb 10:1, 4-10).

Paradoxically, it is always in our own and in our neighbor's best interest that we pray, "thy will be done," and that we understand this petition as the upward complement to our outward appeal to others "on behalf of Christ: be reconciled to God!" (2Cor 5:20) We will not wander far from the will of God if we, in our specific situations, do as Epaphras did, who was "always wrestling in his prayers" on behalf of the Colossian Christians, so that they would "stand mature and fully assured in everything that God wills" (Col 4:12). He it was who taught the gospel to them and reported to Paul and Timothy their "love in the Spirit," which gave Paul occasion to write with such joy:

> we have heard of your faith in Christ Jesus and of the love that you have for all the saints, because of the hope laid up for you in heaven. You have heard of this hope before in the word of the truth, the gospel that has come to you. Just as it is bearing fruit and growing in the whole world, so it has been bearing fruit among yourselves from the day you heard it and truly comprehended the grace of God ... For this reason, since the day we heard it, we have not ceased praying for you and asking that you may be filled with the knowledge of God's will in all spiritual wisdom and understanding (Col 1:4-9).

In short, we can gather from Paul's logic that, in the Spirit, faith, hope, love, and truth are themselves capable of bearing good fruit and spreading the gospel throughout the world, which fruitfulness in turn occasions Paul's petition that those for whom he prays would grow in and "be filled with the knowledge of God's will." In other words, we do not need to, nor can we, seek knowledge of God's specific will for our lives *before* we can be fruitful in the exercise of our faith, hope, and love, or in our receiving the word of truth. Rather, these are grounded in, emerge from, and are measured according to God's sovereign plan, in the same way that, in eternal, spiritual terms, many branches abide in the one True Vine (John 15), and diverse fruits grow from the one tree of life (Rev 22:2).

I. The Heidelberg Catechism (HC) [LORD'S DAY 49]

Q.124. What is the third petition?

A. "Thy will be done, on earth as it is in heaven." That is: grant that we and all men may renounce our own will and obey thy will, which alone is good, without grumbling, so that everyone may carry out his office and calling as willingly and faithfully as the angels in heaven (*BOC*, HC 4.124).

II. Westminster Shorter Catechism (WSC)

Q.103. What do we pray for in the third petition?

A. In the third petition, which is, "Thy will be done in earth, as it is in heaven," we pray that God, by his grace, would make us able and willing to know, obey, and submit to his will in all things (Ps 119:35-36; Acts 21:14), *as the angels do in heaven* (Ps 103:20-22) (*BOC*, WSC 7.103).

III. Westminster Larger Catechism (WLC)

Q.192. What do we pray for in the third petition?

A. In the third petition (which is, "Thy will be done on earth as it is in heaven") (Matt 6:10), *acknowledging that by nature we and all men are not only utterly unable and unwilling to know and do the will of God* (1Cor 2:14; Rom 8:5, 8), *but prone to rebel against his Word* (Rom 8:7), *to repine and murmur against his providence* (Matt 20:11-12; Ps 73:3), *and wholly inclined to do the will of the flesh, and of the devil* (Titus 3:3; Eph 2:2-3)*: we pray that God would by his Spirit take away from ourselves and others all blindness* (Eph 1:17-18), *weakness* (Eph 3:16), *indisposedness* (Matt 26:40-41; Rom 7:24-25), *and perverseness of heart* (Ezek 11:19; Jer 31:18), *and by his grace make us able and willing to know, do, and submit to his will in all things* (Ps 119:35; Acts 21:14; 1Sam 3:18), *with the like humility* (Ps 123:2; 131:2; Mic 6:8), *cheerfulness* (Ps 100:2), *faithfulness* (Isa 38:3; Eph 6:6), *diligence* (Ps 119:4), *zeal* (Rom 12:11), *sincerity* (2Cor 1:12), *and constancy* (Ps 119:112; Rom 2:7), *as the angels do in heaven* (Ps 103:20-22; Dan 7:10) (*BOC*, WLC 7.302).

4. The Fourth Petition:

"Give us this day our daily bread" (Matthew 6:11)

Τὸν ἄρτον ἡμῶν τὸν ἐπιούσιον δὸς ἡμῖν σήμερον

This is the most difficult petition to translate. The most problematic word, ἐπιούσιον, is traditionally rendered *daily*. The word is rare; thus, its precise meaning is a matter of some debate. Origen claimed the word was coined by the evangelists and/or is original to the gospels. Luz summarizes the options with five possible interpretations, though his adjudication between them is not entirely compelling:

(1) Christological (Eucharistic) interpretation: Origen interpreted ούσια as ***substance***; the bread is that which unites with our substance; our bodies absorb it and its nutrients become part of our body and we are transformed thereby. According to a popular saying: "You are what you eat." Jerome translated the word into Latin as *supersubstantialis*

("substance from above").[22] As we eat "the body of Christ," we take Christ into us, and we the church become in turn "the body of Christ."

(2) Aristotelian interpretation: ἐπι = *for* + οὐσια = ***existence*** (see *Parts of Animals*). We are asking for the bread that is necessary for our existence or sustenance; in other words, ordinary bread.

(3) Understood as a reference to manna in the wilderness (Exod 16), a related word [ἐπιούσῃ] signifying the *next* or *following* day, or *tomorrow* (Acts 7:26; 16:11; 20:15; 21:18; 23:11) may be in use here, which would indicate an allusion to the need for the Israelites to pray, specifically on Fridays, for the manna they were prohibited from collecting on the Sabbath (Saturday). Obviously, Christian interpretation would view this text in very close relation to Christological/Eucharistic bread, above (1), as well as to the heavenly banquet, below (5).

(4) Luz prefers the simple translation: *Give us today our bread* ***for tomorrow***. This is supported by the early Christian *Gospel of the Nazoreans*.

(5) Finally, the bread mentioned may be "*future*" bread, the bread of the eschatological, heavenly banquet (Mark 14:25; Matt 8:11f; Luke 14:14; 22:30).

But let us look at the word ἐπιούσιον more closely. Again, when used with the accusative case, ἐπι- means ***for*** or ***towards***. It is noteworthy that Stoic philosophy understood οὐσιον as ***eternal being***. Quite possibly this bread is to be understood as *nourishment for eternal life*, that is, in the Christological/Eucharistic sense (1), which itself is a fulfillment of the Exodus manna tradition (3), but a foretaste of the eschatological banquet (5). Interestingly, John 6:30-32 brings together the manna tradition of Exodus 16 with Christ's feeding of the multitude in the wilderness with the miraculous multiplication of the loaves and fishes (John 6:1-14), by way of the assertion that Jesus himself is the living bread, sent from God, which endures for eternal life (6:26-29, 32-40). Jesus is speaking of this heavenly bread, speaking of himself, when he says: "Those who eat my flesh and drink my blood have eternal life, and I will raise them up on the last day" (John 6:54).

But there is another sense to the feminine word ούσια as it occurs in scripture, namely in Luke's parable of the prodigal son (Luke 15:3-32). The plain meaning of the term there is *property* or *wealth*, or in this particular instance, the *inheritance*. We must be cautious here, because we certainly do not want to encourage the prodigal squandering of the inheritance that we see in the younger son, especially in his form of dissolute living. But there is a positive sense we might derive from once again recalling that we are praying to our Father as "sons" and co-heirs with Christ, himself the bread of life. Again, this is not in any way to warrant a materialistic interpretation, but to remind us of our proper relation to our heavenly Father, who gives readily to his younger son all that he asks for and who says to his older son: "All that I have is yours."

To the extent that wealth or treasure is intended, this would not be earthly treasure which rust and moth consume [βρῶσις], but the opposite of that, namely, the heavenly treasure or reward that is gained by earthly generosity (Matt 6:19-20; 19:21; Mark 10:21; Luke 12:33; 18:22; Jas 5:3). In this sense, the phrase that includes the *neologism* coined here in The Lord's Prayer is quite possibly another deliberately mixed metaphor which should read: *begin to give us this day* [δὸς ἡμῖν σήμερον] ... *our bread for/unto (heavenly) substance/treasure* [Τὸν ἄρτον ἡμῶν τὸν ἐπιούσιον (m. acc.)].

Before we dismiss this novel reading, an admittedly awkward rendering, consider what Jesus said when his disciples found him in conversation with the Samaritan woman at Jacob's well, specifically, where he speaks of his unknown food, his secret bread, or his "hidden manna" (Rev 2:17):

> Meanwhile the disciples were urging him, "Rabbi, eat something." But he said to them, "I have food to eat that you do not know about ['Εγὼ βρῶσιν ἔχω φαγεῖν ἣν ὑμεῖς ούκ οἴδατε]." So the disciples said to one another, "Surely no one has brought him something to eat?" Jesus said to them, "My food is to do the will of him who sent me and to complete his work ['Εμὸν βρῶμά ἐστιν ἵνα ποιήσω τὸ θέλημα τοῦ πέμψαντός με καὶ τελειώσω αὐτοῦ τὸ ἔργον]" (John 4:31-34).

In the end there is nothing to prevent us from an inclusive reading that takes account of all these senses, especially considering the fact that we are appealing to our heavenly Father who is generous to provide *all* that we need. God knows we need temporal sustenance, as well as provisions for the future, especially if we are to keep the Sabbath holy. But, as Strecker and Dean observe,[23] it is for this very reason that Jesus tells us *not* to worry about what we shall eat, but to put first things first, namely, the kingdom of God and his righteousness (Matt 6:25-34). Since we are specifically instructed not to worry about tomorrow, why then, we might ask, should we pray for our bread for tomorrow? God has sent Christ to be our living bread which endures for eternity, the body of Christ we receive in the Lord's Supper, itself a foretaste of the heavenly banquet. What we have added to our interpretive possibilities is the appeal that we might be fed with the bread that yields treasure in heaven, namely, the doing of the Father's will on earth as it is done in heaven! This would suggest, in many ways, that the third and the fourth petitions of the Lord's Prayer are in fact asking for the same thing. Thus we might paraphrase both petitions in this way:

> *... thy will be done on earth as it is in heaven, and give us this day our share in doing thy will on earth that we might be fed with heavenly manna and store up for ourselves treasure in heaven.*

What is perhaps most interesting about this interpretation is the way in which it is borne out in Jesus' manner of recapitulation as he comments on the prayer in the verses that follow.

Let us consider this in more detail and survey the structure of the prayer once again in relation to its setting, since, with the fourth petition we have in a sense crossed the threshold from the *thy*-petitions to the *we*-petitions, from the first table of the covenent to the second.

If the first and sixth petitions, which hallow the Father's name (6:9) and ask for deliverance from the evil one (6:13), may be seen as bookends to the prayer, these may be seen to be restated in the summary reminder that we cannot serve two masters (6:24). Otherwise, what immediately follows the prayer itself is a gloss (6:14-15) on the fifth petition on forgiveness (6:12). Should we not then look for a similar gloss on the fourth petition for bread (6:11) in Jesus' comments on fasting in secret (6:16-18)? In fact, in John 4, Jesus had not eaten temporal bread, but was apparently fasting from it precisely when he said that he had the bread of doing the will of the Father. Likewise, we should not be surprised that what follows the teaching on fasting is a commentary that continues drawing the distinction between heaven and earth, which in the third petition concerns doing God's will (6:10) and in the commentary concerns storing up treasure (6:19-21). Finally, this would lead us to correlate the second petition, "thy kingdom come" (6:10), with what Jesus has to say about the eye being lamp of the body which either fills the whole body with light if the eye is healthy, or with darkness if it is unhealthy (6:22-23). In other words, each of these sections that follow The Lord's Prayer might well be seen to be a commentary (in reverse order) on the petitions. In which case, the commentary on the bread petition would plainly show that *what we have been asking for is not temporal bread at all, but that which involves secret fasting and, I would suggest, doing the will of the Father.* "For we are what he has made us, created in Christ Jesus for good works, which God prepared beforehand to be our way of life" (Eph 2:10).

Of course there is much more to be said about the bread metaphor in scripture, especially as it relates to the seed/word of God and to the eucharistic fellowship.[24] Here it will suffice to say that the notion of hidden manna (Rev 2:17) recalls the three things contained in the ark of the covenant: "a golden urn holding the manna, and Aaron's rod that budded, and the tablets of the covenant" (Heb 9:4). In other words, the metaphor places this heavenly bread in extremely close proximity to the word of God or the tablets of the covenant, and in a way that is entirely consistent with the biblical witness: "one does not live by bread alone, but by every word that comes from the mouth of the LORD" (Deut 8:3; Matt 4:4; Luke 4:4). It also places it in intimate relation to the fruitful almond bough with its priestly and prophetic (visually oracular) connotations, almonds being a classic symbol for the eye by virtue of their shape.

I. The Heidelberg Catechism (HC) [LORD'S DAY 50]

Q.125. What is the fourth petition?

A. *"Give us this day our daily bread." That is: be pleased to provide for all our bodily needs so that thereby we may acknowledge that thou art the only source of all that is good, and that without thy blessing neither our care and labor nor thy gifts can do us any good. Therefore, may we withdraw our trust from all creatures and place it in thee alone* (BOC, HC 4.125).

II. Westminster Shorter Catechism **(WSC)**

Q.104. What do we pray for in the fourth petition?

A. *In the fourth petition, which is, "Give us this day our daily bread," we pray that, of God's free gift, we may receive a competent portion of the good things of this life* (Prov 30:8), *and enjoy his blessing with them* (1Tim 4:4-5; Prov 10:22) (*BOC*, WSC 7.104).

III. Westminster Larger Catechism (WLC)

Q.193. What do we pray for in the fourth petition?

A. *In the fourth petition (which is, "Give us this day our daily bread")* (Matt 6:11), *acknowledging that in Adam, and by our own sin, we have forfeited our right to all the outward blessings of this life, and deserve to be wholly deprived of them by God, and to have them cursed to us in the use of them* (Gen 3:17; Lam 3:22; Deut 28:15-68); *and that neither they of themselves are able to sustain us* (Deut 8:3), *nor we to merit* (Gen 32:10), *or by our own industry to procure them* (Deut 8:18; Prov 10:22), *but prone to desire* (Luke 12:15; Jer 6:13), *get* (Hos 12:7), *and use them unlawfully* (Jas 4:3): *we pray for ourselves and others, that both they and we, waiting upon the providence of God from day today in the use of lawful means may,of his free gift, and as to his fatherly wisdom shall seem best, enjoy a competent portion of them* (Gen 28:20-21; Jas 4:13, 15; Ps 90:17; 144:12-15), *and have the same continued and blessed unto us in our holy and comfortable use of them* (1Tim 4:4-5; Prov 10:22), *and contentment in them* (1Tim 6:6, 8); *and be kept from all things that are contrary to our temporal support and comfort* (Prov 30:8-9) (*BOC*, WLC 7.303).

5. The Fifth Petition:

"And forgive us our debts as we forgive our debtors"

(Matthew 6:12)

καὶ ἄφες ἡμῖν τὰ ὀφειλήματα ἡμῶν
ὡς καὶ ἡμεῖς ἀφήκαμεν τοῖς ὀφειλέταις ἡμῶν

With regard to the fourth petition, we referred to the parable of the prodigal son, and specifically to the way in which the father in that parable dealt with his sons. The prodigal son returned fully aware that he was much in his father's debt, having squandered half of the estate. Indeed, his statement, "I am no longer worthy to be called your son" (Luke 15:19, 21), indicates a shift in categories to which we must pay careful attention. The son confesses that he has "sinned against heaven and before you" (Luke 15:21). His conviction is unmitigated. Heaven and earth, or at least his earthly family members, have seen his worthless behavior, his squandering of his inheritance. He can no longer allow himself to think according to the category of family, but can only hope to be treated "like one of (the) hired hands" (15:19). His family relationship of love and grace is lost to him. He hopes only for an employment contract. The difference is the same as that between a gift given and wages earned (Rom 4:4). In terms of Kierkegaard's existential stages, he has lapsed from the sphere of *faith*, where negotations take place around the dinner table, to the sphere of *esthetics* (consumption) where he lived as a self-indulgent playboy and a glutton, until he "came to himself" and realized his guilt, i.e., by rising into the intermediate sphere of the *ethics*, where negotiations are formal, contractual, subject to litigation in the civil courts. Yet even here, he remained far below the sphere of *faith* whence he had fallen.

But how shameful it is for people of faith to go to court "and before unbelievers at that." To do so is "already a defeat," so "Why not rather be wronged? Why not rather be defrauded?" (1Cor 6:1-7). This apparent ignoring, or ignorance, of his right to punitive action or civil litigation in the ethical sphere is precisely what we see in the father's response to the prodigal son. He does not enter with his son into the (lower!) ethical sphere by speaking of legal debts or employment contracts. Rather, he accords to the prodigal the higher honors of sonship — the robe, the ring, the sandals, the fatted calf, the celebratory feast — and he restores him to the (higher) sphere of faith. Likewise, Deuteronomy draws a clear distinction between how, every seventh year, Israel was to settle its claims against the alien versus how they were to remit the debts of a member of the community:

> Every seventh year you shall grant a remission of debts. And this is the manner of the remission: every creditor shall remit the claim that is held against a neighbor, not exacting it of a neighbor who is a member of the community, because the Lord's remission has been proclaimed. Of a foreigner you may exact it, but you must remit your claim on whatever any member of your community owes you (Deut 15:1-3; cf. Exod 21:2).

Here, the LORD's gracious remission is the pattern for the conduct of members of the covenant fellowship toward one another, just as the prodigal's father deals with his *penitent* son according to "grace through faith" (Eph 2:9-10) rather than through any legal recourse that would obtain outside the covenant bonds of familial and communal love.

This brief consideration of the parable of the prodigal son not only reminds us that we continue to address our petitions to our heavenly Father, but also illustrates how, in doing so, we allow certain categories to emerge by which we can interpret the terminology used in the prayer. Let us turn our attention to four terms: *forgiveness*, *debts*, *trespasses*, and the ambiguous, but relational term, *as*.

i. "forgive." The word here literally means *to cancel*. It bears the negating prefix, *a-*. The noun ἄφεσις means *remission* (occuring 32 times in *Greek Textus Receptus*), and the related verb ἀφιέναι or ἀφιέιν means *to remit* or *to relinquish* (occuring 132 times in *GTR*).

The word is used in relation to various direct objects. In Luke's version of this petition, it is used with respect to *sins*, although the latter part of the petition correlates *sins*, in parallel fashion, with the notion of *indebtedness*: "And forgive us our sins, for we ourselves forgive everyone indebted to us" (11:4). Luke-Acts is particularly notable for the frequency with which *"forgiveness of sins"* [ἄφεσιν ἁμαρτιῶν] is mentioned (Luke 1:77; 3:3; 24:47; Acts 2:38; 5:31; 10:43; 13:38; 26:18), though the phrase does occur elsewhere, perhaps most importantly, in relation to baptism and the Lord's Supper (Mark 1:4; Matt 26:28). Particularly interesting, in light of our discussion of the parable of the prodigal, is what the Father has done for us in Christ with respect to the *forgiveness of sins*. "He has rescued us from the power of darkness and transferred us into the kingdom of his beloved Son, in whom we have redemption, the forgiveness of sins" (Col 1:14). As with the father's gracious reception in the parable, we see that there is involved what amounts to a transfer between two spheres, a transfer that entails the *cancellation of debt* (i.e. literally, a *re-deeming*) and the *forgiveness of sins*. In what follows, we will see, again and again, how the New Testament defines the one in terms of the other. But first let us name the exceptions to this general rule.

Occasionally, the verb is used of people (Matt 18:35; Luke 23:34), but this tends to be rather more an abbreviated way of saying that we *forgive the sins of* people or *cancel the debts for* people. Frequently, the word English word *forgive*, when applied to people, refers to another word meaning *to be gracious toward* them [χαριζειν; cf. Col 3:13]. Simply put, forgiveness does not cancel *people*, it cancels their *debts*, their *sins*.

Sometimes, Jesus uses the verb without any specific direct object (Luke 17:3-4), but what he does make quite specific is that we are to forgive *every* time a sinner repents.

One most interesting occurrence of the verb is at Jesus' baptism, where he answers John's protest that he should be baptized by Jesus, not the other way around: "*Permit* it now, for it is proper in this way to fulfill all righteousness" (Matt 3:15). Thus *remittance* is akin to *permission*, to *relinquishment*, to taking the passive approach and *allowing something to happen*. An often overlooked parable in Luke offers yet another good example:

> "A man had a fig tree planted in his vineyard; and he came looking for fruit on it and found none. So he said to the gardener, 'See here! For three years I have come looking for fruit on this fig tree, and still I find none. Cut it down! Why should it be wasting the soil?' He replied, 'Sir, *let it alone* for one more year, until I dig around it and put manure on it. If it bears fruit next year, well and good; but if not, you can cut it down'" (Luke 13:6-9)

It is in this sense that the verb is sometimes used in association with reconciliation, but is not used for the act of reconciliation itself:

> "*leave* your gift there before the altar and go; first be reconciled to your brother or sister, and then come and offer your gift" (Matt 5:24); "if anyone wants to sue you and take your coat, *give* your cloak as well" (5:40); "Or how can you say to your neighbor, '*Let* me take the speck out of your eye,' while the log is in your own eye?'" (7:4; Luke 6:42).

Most often, however, the word is used in relation to debts or financial obligations. In fact, the noun of which the verb [ἀφιέιν] is a negation, is the cognate word for *debt* [ὀφειλή]. It is not surprising that, of the four evangelists, Luke uses the word most frequently, who gives greatest emphasis to proclaiming good news to the poor. The verb occurs twice in the passage from Isaiah that Jesus reads in the synagogue in Nazareth to inaugurate his earthly ministry (Luke 4:18-19; Isa 61:1). We will look more closely at the synonymous relation between the forgiveness of sins and the cancellation of debts in the section to follow, but before we do so, three important concepts must be mentioned which relate to the forgiveness of sins.

First, there is the sobering question of the unforgivable sin: "whoever blasphemes against the Holy Spirit can never have forgiveness, but is guilty of an eternal sin" (Mark 3:29). This is an extremely alarming text that should certainly awaken in us the only legitimate fear, namely, the fear of "him who, after he has killed, has authority to cast into hell. Yes, I tell you, fear him!" (Luke 12:5). What may help us to understand and heed this warning is the fact that Jesus lays it at the feet of the scribes from Jerusalem who charge: "He has Beelzebul, and by the ruler of the demons he casts out demons" (Mark 3:22). Jesus, however, challenges them by restating their charge in the clearest terms possible: "How can Satan cast out Satan?" (Mark 3:23). In other words, Jesus has just done a good deed of power by the Holy Spirit, yet the scribes are on the verge of blaspheming the Holy Spirit by attributing this good deed to the evil one. They "call evil good and good evil, ... put darkness for light and light for darkness, ... put bitter for sweet and sweet for bitter!" (Isa 5:20) Such is the nature of the unforgivable sin. God is gracious and will forgive people "for their sins and whatever blasphemies they utter" (Mark 3:29), but not the blasphemy against the Holy Spirit. About this unforgivable sin, it is best to avoid saying too much or interpreting it too fully. What we can affirm, however, is what we observed in our consideration of the third petition, namely, that while God wills that none should perish, but that all should come to repentance and faith, nevertheless, God does not guarantee that all will come. Christ and the Spirit are given to us as our guarantee, but those who blaspheme the Holy Spirit thus reject the guarantee, the very gift of faith by which the offer of salvation has been extended to them.

Second, an extremely important passage in the Epistle to the Hebrews (9:1-10:39) explains that, "without the shedding of blood there is no forgiveness of sins" (9:22). Yet, we are also promised that Christ has "offered for all time a single sacrifice for sins," after which "he sat down at the right hand of God" (10:12). Thus, while forgiveness required blood atonement, which Christ was able to provide, he being both our sinless high priest (4:15) and the holy "lamb of God who takes away the sin of the world" (John 1:29, 36), nevertheless, this atonement has been made once and for all (Rom 6:10; Heb 7:27; 9:12, 26; 10:2, 10; 1Pet 3:18). His sacrifice is *never* to be repeated: "Where there is forgiveness ... there is no longer any offering for sin" (Heb 10:18).

Third and finally, we do well to remember the promise of God's gracious response to our confession of sins, which is also described in the welcome of the father of the prodigal: "If we confess our sins, he who is faithful and just will forgive us our sins and cleanse us from all unrighteousness" (1John 1:9).

We can summarize these three important texts in this way: God has provided a sure and certain, but also a singular and unique, way of salvation by the once and for all sacrifice of Christ on the cross, but as quick and faithful as God is to forgive, it is literally un-forgivable to blaspheme the spirit of forgiveness, the Holy Spirit, the very goodness of God by which we are forgiven and saved. Thus, there is no guarantee of salvation for those who spurn the guarantee itself, and there is no forgiveness for those who, to the end, despise forgiveness itself.

ii. "our debts." But what shall we make of this odd choice of financial terminology: *debts* [ὀφειλήματα] and *debtors* [ὀφειλέταις]? Three parables are particularly important for understanding the fifth petition in terms of the cancellation of debts. The first one, the Parable of the Unforgiving Servant (Matt 18:21-35) is framed in terms of *forgiveness of sins* (Matt 18:21, 35), but the parable itself (18:23-34) is couched in terms of the *cancellation of debts* (18:27, 30, 32, 34). We will consider this parable in more detail below as we turn to the need for mutual, reciprocal forgiveness. Meanwhile, two parables in Luke also serve to explain the forgiveness of *sins* by way of the cancellation (or the reduction) of *debts*. The first of these two (Luke 7:36-50) is told with an almost identical structure to that of the unforgiving servant (Matt 18:21-35). Jesus is invited to eat in the house of a Pharisee. While he is there a woman "who was a sinner" comes and bathes his feet with her tears (Luke 7:36-37). The host is offended that Jesus receives this gesture from this woman, for again, the host thinks, "she is a sinner" (Luke 7:39-40). Jesus then tells a parable of a creditor who cancelled the debts for two people, one of whose debt was ten times that of the other. The Pharisee rightly concludes that the one released from the greater debt will love the creditor more (7:40-43). Finally, Jesus interprets the parable by shifting back from the category of the cancellation of debts to that of the forgiveness of sins. The sins of the woman, "which were many, have been forgiven; hence she has shown great love. But the one to whom little is forgiven, loves little" (7:47). Jesus goes on to inform the woman that her sins are forgiven, while "those who were at the table with him began to say among themselves, 'Who is this who even forgives sins?'" (7:48-49). In short, this parable too is framed in terms of forgiveness of sins, while the parable itself unfolds in terms of the cancellation of debts.

Another very important feature of this parable may help us to understand Jesus' use of monetary (quantitative) metaphor. Notice that the issue of sin, viewed from a human perspective (that of the Pharisee and those gathered at the table with Jesus), is seen to be a qualitative distinction. The Pharisee is righteous or "good" in his own eyes, and the woman is sinful or "bad." Good and bad are obviously opposite qualities, as are righteousness and sinfulness, as are (recalling the first petition) the holy and the common, purity and impurity. The effect of Jesus' parable is to toss the Pharisee over the wall, so to speak, that marks the "infinite qualitative difference" between good and bad, to place him into a zone where the only difference between the Pharisee and the woman is "quantitative," the sort of difference that can be measured in degrees, or in money, for that matter. We recall that "there is only one who is good" (Matt 19:17), God alone. Between humans, there are only degrees of indebtedness, but everyone is indebted to God. This will help us to understand our third parable.

And we need all the help we can get. This third parable, the parable of the dishonest manager, figures among the most difficult in the gospels. Indeed, at first glance, it almost seems to commend dishonesty. A rich man demands an accounting of his manager, whom, he has learned, has been "squandering his property" (Luke 16:1). Knowing he is about to be fired (16:2), the manager instructs the rich man's debtors to change the amount they owe on their bills, so that "people may welcome me into their homes" (16:3-7). Surprisingly, "his master commended the dishonest manager because he acted shrewdly" (16:8a); thus Jesus summarizes: "make friends for yourselves by means of dishonest wealth [μαμωνᾶ], so that when it is gone, they may welcome you into the eternal homes" (16:9). How are we to make sense of this?

First, the news that spurs the manager to action is that his time is up, the accounting must be rendered. As mortals in relation to the immortal God, we can also avail ourselves of the eschatological stimulus that our own "time limit" is capable of providing us, if we would but consider our mortality soberly and realistically: "teach us to count our days that we may gain a wise heart" (Ps 90:12). We will say more about this below, as we consider the inherent reminder of our mortality that lies at the heart of the synonymous word *trespass*.

Second, notice that *mammon* too will one day be gone, unlike the eternal God. Following this parable, as well as in the Sermon on the Mount (Matt 6:24), we are told that we cannot serve both God and mammon, but here it is clear that mammon *can* serve us. Even though "money can't buy me love" (Lennon and McCartney), nevertheless, by practicing generosity on earth, we can show "good will toward men," and open up new possibilities for human relations, relations that may foster loyalty (1Sam 22:2) and even endure into eternity.

Third, notice the presupposition behind the parable, namely, that the manager is working with property that is not his own. Everything he has to work with belongs to another, to whom he is accountable. The correlation to our own situation before God should be obvious:

> "The earth is the LORD's and all that is in it, the world, and those who live in it" (Ps 24:1). "The land shall not be sold in perpetuity, for the land is mine; with me you are but aliens and tenants" (Lev 25:23).

Fourth, the property that does not belong to the manager either includes or is described *in toto* as dishonest gain. But in what sense is the rich man's working capital to be viewed as the manager's dishonest gain? Perhaps the best explanation for this odd cooking of the books is that the dishonest manager was overcharging the customers in the first place, that an inflated "accounts receivable" figure was shown to the rich man, that the rich man realized the manager was having a good time with the extra income. Thus, when he was called on it, the manager then went about putting things right with the customers and amending the books, so that what he then reported to the rich man was a much lower figure for "accounts receivable." What is refreshing and new is that the rich man, while unsurprised at seeing a more conservative estimate of his wealth, does not seem saddened by the knowledge that he is not as wealthy as the inflated numbers had indicated. He would prefer to have a good *reputation* among his clients — *recall the first petition!?* — as one who does not gouge, but deals fairly and generously with them.

Here again, it is important to mark the qualitative difference that persists between, on the one hand, the owner to whom both the manager and the clients are accountable, and on the other hand, those who are in his debt. In the microcosm of the parable, all the property belongs to the rich man. All the other characters are (qualitatively) accountable to him, though compared to one another they are accountable in (quantitatively) differing capacities and degrees.

Thus, as we consider both the upward, vertical component of the fifth petition, "forgive us our debts," and the outward, horizontal component, "as we forgive our debtors," we can conclude that our indebtedness to God is absolute and eternal, while our indebtedness to one another is relative and temporary.

Further, God is interested in our avoiding temporal indebtedness to one another as much as possible, both in terms of owing others (Prov 22:26) and in terms of demanding payment: "lend, expecting nothing in return. Your reward will be great, and you will be children of the Most High" (Luke 6:35). In addition to the Sabbatical "release" (Deut 15:1-6) and the remission prescribed for the Jubilee (Lev 25:10) there are many examples in scripture of the way in which the LORD promises to intervene, and in fact, intervenes to relieve the poor of their debts, through covenant (Neh 10:31), miracle (2Kings 4:7), the threat of judgment (Isa 24:2), and the promise of life given to the righteous (Ezek 18:5-9). This surely accords with God's desire, which we affirmed in view of the second petition, that we live in relative freedom, including freedom from debt.

On the other hand, we can also say that, insofar as we are free both from temporal, financial obligations to one another and from a worldly concern that our debtors pay us what they owe, we are also free to perceive with unclouded vision and acknowledge our infinite indebtedness to God and to voice our gratitude, to "pay" him our worship, our praise, our thanksgiving, our "*living* sacrifice" (Rom 12:1), which taken together consititute the one offering God desires the most (Pss 50; 100, 107, 116, 118, 136; *et al.*), that *total love of God* described in the greatest commandment (Deut 6:4-5; Matt 22:34-40).

The Epistle to the Romans also offers an interesting example of how we are to understand our indebtedness in relative and absolute terms. Where Paul declares his indebtedness "to Greeks and to barbarians, both to the wise and to the foolish" (Rom 1:14), this is a relative indebtedness that finds its source in God, "whom I serve with my spirit by announcing the gospel of his Son" (1:9). The faith of the Roman church is cause for Paul's thanksgiving to God (1:8), and the basis of his certainty that when he sees them, they will be "mutually encouraged by each other's faith" (1:11-12).

Our absolute indebtedness to the Spirit of God is upheld in the pivotal chapter of the epistle and set over against any temporal indebtedness to the flesh; indeed, this is explained in a way that brings together many of the ideas we have seen at work in The Lord's Prayer.

> So then, brothers and sisters, we are debtors, not to the flesh, to live according to the flesh— for if you live according to the flesh, you will die; but if by the Spirit you put to death the deeds of the body, you will live. For all who are led by the Spirit of God are children of God. For you did not receive a spirit of slavery to fall back into fear, but you have received a spirit of adoption. When we cry, "Abba! Father!" it is that very Spirit bearing witness with our spirit that we are children of God, and if children, then heirs, heirs of God and joint heirs with Christ—if, in fact, we suffer with him so that we may also be glorified with him (Rom 8:12-17).

Here the reality of Christian freedom, adoption, childhood, inheritance, and witness are brought together so as to show the beggarly limits of temporal indebtedness.

But, as we have said, the vertical and total love we are to have for God according to the great commandment will, if it is genuine, issue in neighbor love, which carries with it certain "obligations" that are not merely financial. We will recognize the second commandment, which is like and proceeds from the greatest, where Paul reminds us of our ethical responsibilities:

> Pay to all what is due them—taxes to whom taxes are due, revenue to whom revenue is due, respect to whom respect is due, honor to whom honor is due. Owe no one anything, except to love one another; for the one who loves another has fulfilled the law (Rom 13:7-8).

Further, these responsibilities are not ethical in the worldly spirit of competition, but they are of that peculiar form of Christian ethics which testifies to Christ's solidarity with and investment in the weak and the humble: "We who are strong ought to put up with the failings of the weak, and not to please ourselves. Each of us must please our neighbor for the good purpose of building up the neighbor. For Christ did not please himself; but, as it is written, 'The insults of those who insult you have fallen on me'" (Rom 15:1-3). The Christian's ethical obligation in human relations, in every case, may be traced back to the one absolute relation and obligation to God.

We see this again where Philemon's indebtedness to Paul for the bringing him the gospel of eternal salvation outweighs any worldly obligation that Paul might incur to Philemon as a result of his appeal to the slaveowner to grant Onesimus his freedom. "If he has wronged you in any way, or owes you anything, charge that to my account. I, Paul, am writing this with my own hand: I will repay it. I say nothing about your owing me even your own self" (Philemon 18-19). Paul, of course, asks that the liberation of Onesimus not be one granted in merely temporal, legal terms, but in the familial spirit of Christian faith and good will:

> I preferred to do nothing without your consent, in order *that your good deed might be voluntary and not something forced.* Perhaps this is the reason he was separated from you for a while, so that you might have him back forever, *no longer as a slave but more than a slave, a beloved brother*—especially to me but how much more to you, *both in the flesh and in the Lord* (14-16).

Much more could be said regarding the ethical obligations that the Christian life entails. But we must conclude our consideration of the peculiar financial metaphor, *debts*, in terms of which these obligations are couched in the fifth petition with the observation that the distinctions we have clarified above are still in effect.

iii. "trespass." In treating the fourth petition, we said that the verses that follow The Lord's Prayer serve as a commentary on the petitions themselves, beginning with the fifth petition, as found in the first words following the prayer: "For if you forgive others their trespasses, your heavenly Father will also forgive you; but if you do not forgive others, neither will your Father forgive your trespasses" (Matt 6:14-15). Here the object of forgiveness is *not* debts, but *trespasses* [παραπτώματα = παρα (*next to,* w. acc.) + πτώματα (*corpse*)]. While it is beyond the scope of our immediate task to investigate thoroughly the notion of trespasses, we should note briefly that the word *trespass* has at its core the awareness of our *mortality*. In recognizing the mortality of our debtors, of those who trespass against us, surely we can identify with their fragility and mortality and be reminded of our own mortality. Everyone who has trespassed is παραπτώματα: *"all but* (or *nigh unto) a corpse."* Who cannot say with Paul, "Wretched man that I am! Who will rescue me from this body of death?" (Rom 7:24). Surely we too are "always carrying in the body the death of Jesus" (2Cor 4:10). In light of the impending death of our debtors and in light of our own mortaility — "it is appointed for mortals to die once, and after that the judgment" (Heb 9:27) — we are forced to ask ourselves: is the refusal to forgive those who have trespassed against us, is our condemnation of them, really worth it in light of the eternal consequences? Clearly not! Yet it falls to each one to make this determination for oneself. For those who deny the necessity of forgiveness, or withhold forgiveness from others, the unforgivable sin and its gloomy results loom on the horizon: "judgment will be without mercy to anyone who has shown no mercy" (Jas 2:13a). But for the merciful, "mercy triumphs over judgment" (Jas 2:13b). We know that "whoever keeps the whole law but fails in one point has become accountable for all of it" (Jas 2:10). Further, we know that "the wages of sin is death" (Rom 6:23a), thus even the slightest trangression against God's holiness earns us the status of corpse. But again, in The Lord's Prayer, we do not address God as our employer from whom the most we can hope to receive is the wages we are due; rather, we address as our heavenly Father from whom "the free gift of God is eternal life in Christ Jesus our Lord" (Rom 6:23b). Even in the light of the capital sentence facing those who trangress, we may still sing with Paul the great doxology with which he opens his Epistle to the Ephesians:

> Blessed be the God and Father of our Lord Jesus Christ, who has blessed us in Christ with every spiritual blessing in the heavenly places, just as he chose us in Christ before the foundation of the world to be holy and blameless before him in love. *He destined us for adoption as his children through Jesus Christ, according to the good pleasure of his will*, to the praise of his glorious grace that he freely bestowed on us in the Beloved. *In him we have redemption through his blood, the forgiveness of our trespasses, according to the riches of his grace that he lavished on us.* With all wisdom and insight *he has made known to us the mystery of his will, according to his good pleasure*

> *that he set forth in Christ, as a plan for the fullness of time, to gather up all things in him, things in heaven and things on earth. In Christ we have also obtained an inheritance, having been destined according to the purpose of him who accomplishes all things according to his counsel and will,* so that we, who were the first to set our hope on Christ, might live for the praise of his glory. *In him you also, when you had heard the word of truth, the gospel of your salvation, and had believed in him, were marked with the seal of the promised Holy Spirit; this is the pledge of our inheritance toward redemption as God's own people, to the praise of his glory* (Eph 1:3-14).

iv. "as we forgive our debtors." Throughout this chapter, we have been reminded that forgiveness of sins, or the cancellation of debts, is to be given and practiced, freely and mutually. Luke's version of this petition presupposes, and makes our being forgiven contingent upon, our forgiveness of others: "And forgive us our sins, for we ourselves forgive everyone indebted to us" (Luke 11:4).

Further, we have noted that a great deal depends on our forgiving others thoroughly. Indeed, one passage even suggests that our failure to forgive can actually *impede* the heavenly Father's forgiving us!

> "Whenever you stand praying, forgive, if you have anything against anyone; so that your Father in heaven may also forgive you your trespasses" (Mark 11:25; cf. Luke 6:37)

Thus, while absolute indebtedness characterizes our relation to God and relative indebtedness our relation to our neighbors, the forgiveness and reconciliation we have the power to give within the relative sphere of human relations effects how forthcoming God will be in forgiving our sins. We are to be reconciled in our neighbor relations *before* we meet the divine judge who has absolute authority over our destiny:

> "So when you are offering your gift at the altar, if you remember that your brother or sister has something against you, leave your gift there before the altar and go; first be reconciled to your brother or sister, and then come and offer your gift. Come to terms quickly with your accuser while you are on the way to court with him, or your accuser may hand you over to the judge, and the judge to the guard, and you will be thrown into prison. Truly I tell you, you will never get out until you have paid the last penny" (Matt 5:23-26).

Surely the stakes are extremely high, and nothing must be allowed to make us stingy and begrudging with the forgiveness that others need, and of which we ourselves are no less in need. Nothing can make this clearer than the parable of the unforgiving servant:

> Then Peter came and said to him, "Lord, if another member of the church sins against me, how often should I forgive? As many as seven times?" Jesus said to him, "Not seven times, but, I tell you, seventy-seven times. "For this reason the kingdom of heaven may be compared to a king who wished to settle accounts with his slaves. When he began the reckoning, one who owed him ten thousand talents was brought to him; and, as he could not pay, his lord ordered him to be sold, together with his wife and children and all his possessions, and payment to be made. So the slave fell on his knees before him, saying, 'Have patience with me, and I will pay you everything.' And out of pity for him, the lord of that slave released him and forgave him the debt. But that same slave, as he went out, came upon one of his fellow slaves who

> owed him a hundred denarii; and seizing him by the throat, he said, 'Pay what you owe.' Then his fellow slave fell down and pleaded with him, 'Have patience with me, and I will pay you.' But he refused; then he went and threw him into prison until he would pay the debt. When his fellow slaves saw what had happened, they were greatly distressed, and they went and reported to their lord all that had taken place. Then his lord summoned him and said to him, 'You wicked slave! I forgave you all that debt because you pleaded with me. Should you not have had mercy on your fellow slave, as I had mercy on you?' And in anger his lord handed him over to be tortured until he would pay his entire debt. So my heavenly Father will also do to every one of you, if you do not forgive your brother or sister from your heart" (Matt 18:21-35).

In light of these severe consequences, we must not miss the great weight of that seemingly innocuous statement: "*as* we forgive our debtors." The highly ambiguous word "as" is freighted with possible implications that we would do well to consider thoroughly as we offer up the fifth petition: "*at precisely the same time that* we forgive our debtors;" "*to the same degree that* we forgive them;" "*with the same measure* (Matt 7:2) that we forgive them;" "*with the same sincerity and thoroughness with which* we forgive them;" or perhaps most simply, "*if* we forgive our debtors." Let us not belabor the point, but simply reiterate that the consequences are sobering and severe where we fail to forgive, but where we do forgive, the benefits are enormous.

v. The authority to forgive and the power of the keys. It is for this reason that we must deal directly with the objection raised by various religious persons in the gospels when they encounter Jesus, as the Son of Man, exercising his "authority on earth to forgive sins" (Mark 2:10; Matt 9:2-8; Luke 5:17-26). We must answer those who heard him declare forgiveness (Luke 7:48) and salvation by faith (7:50) to the sinful woman and who asked: "Who is this who even forgives sins?" (Luke 7:49).

The prevailing assumption under which they labor who ask such a question is that God alone can forgive sins. Indeed, those scribes who heard Jesus forgive the paralytic, were so convinced of this that they cried: "Why does this fellow speak in this way? It is blasphemy! Who can forgive sins but God alone?" (Mark 2:7). In fact, the scribes had solid scriptural evidence to support their assumption (Exod 34:6-7; Isa 43:25; 44:22). But the correctness of the assumption can only serve to affirm the fact that Jesus the God-man (i.e., who is simultaneously and fully the Son of Man and the Son of God) is "God with us," God on earth doing what God alone can do.

Meanwhile, however, the same Immanuel has also authorized and commanded that "repentance and forgiveness of sins is to be proclaimed *in his name* to all nations, beginning from Jerusalem" (Luke 24:47). Further, he instructs the disciples on three different occasions regarding the administration of what is known in the confessions as "the power of the keys." The first occasion is Peter's confession of Jesus' true identity, a confession that was inspired by the heavenly Father (Matt 16:16-17) and that stands in total contrast to Peter's subsequent, nearly immediate and diabolical, lapse (16:20-23). Jesus responds to Peter's confession, however, in a way that assures us Peter's ensuing lapse was not permanent:

> "And I tell you, you are Peter, and on this rock I will build my church, and the gates of Hades will not prevail against it. I will give you the keys of the kingdom of heaven, and whatever you bind on earth will be bound in heaven, and whatever you loose on earth will be loosed in heaven" (Matt 16:18-19).

Nevertheless, as Luther observed (in his disputation on "The Keys"), the fact that Peter subsequently gives voice to Satan, the stumbling block (16:20-23), should warn us decisively from investing the power of the keys in a single human successor to Peter. Despite the fact that, even today, the papal ensignia of the Bishop of Rome remains the crossed keys, as though the pope alone were invested with the power of the keys, this power is given to all who confess with the inspired, not the lapsed, Peter: "You are the Messiah, the Son of the living God" (Matt 16:16).

Though the keys themselves are not mentioned again in the gospels, their use for binding and loosing is. In fact, the next occasion immediately preceeds the parable of the unforgiving servant, which we have just considered above. The subject of Jesus' discourse is forgiveness, and specifically, church discipline:

> "If another member of the church sins against you, go and point out the fault when the two of you are alone. If the member listens to you, you have regained that one. But if you are not listened to, take one or two others along with you, so that every word may be confirmed by the evidence of two or three witnesses. If the member refuses to listen to them, tell it to the church; and if the offender refuses to listen even to the church, let such a one be to you as a Gentile and a tax collector. Truly I tell you, whatever you bind on earth will be bound in heaven, and whatever you

> loose on earth will be loosed in heaven. Again, truly I tell you, if two of you agree on earth about anything you ask, it will be done for you by my Father in heaven. For where two or three are gathered in my name, I am there among them" (Matt 18:15-20).

Clearly, Christ has authorized not only Peter, but an undesignated "two or three," those who "are gathered in his name," and indeed, "the church," to exercise the binding and loosing use of the keys.

Finally, whereas in Matthew's gospel we are assured that the risen Christ has in fact been given "all authority in heaven and on earth" (Matt 28:18), in John's Pentecostal portrayal of an Easter appearance of the risen Lord, Jesus breathes on the disciples and says to them, "Receive the Holy Spirit. If you forgive the sins of any, they are forgiven them; if you retain the sins of any, they are retained" (John 20:22-23).

Outside of the gospels, Paul's Corinthian correspondence also testifies to the manner in which the church is to pastorally administer the power of the keys and to respect one another's authority to do so, knowing that when it is done, it is done "in the presence of Christ" (2Cor 2:7, 10).

Thus, we have been authorized to forgive by the One from whom all authority derives. If we profess that "Jesus Christ is Lord," then we are authorized to forgive, and to exercise fully and frequently the power of the keys. We have no excuse for holding on to anger, bitterness, or grudge.

But there is another dimension to *the power of the keys*, or *the office of the keys,* in fact, the primary dimension, that we have not mentioned; one that should radically expand our understanding of the fifth petition. That primary dimension is "the preaching of the holy gospel," and as the act of forgiving, it has the power to "open heaven." This is best stated in the words of the Heidelberg Catechism (below). Thus. the preaching of the gospel and the loosing of the bonds of sin by the practice of forgiveness, "the keys," are placed on the tongue and in the hands of all who would proclaim that "Jesus is the Christ, the Son of the Living God!" (Matt 16:16). Further, the power to bind is also entrusted to believers in Christ. But as we have seen, the binding of others in their sins quite possibly limits the degree to which we ourselves can hope and expect to be forgiven. Thus, if the binding of other's sins is to be used at all, it is only with sincere humility, and I would add, much fear and trembling.

I. The Heidelberg Catechism [LORD'S DAY 31]

Q.83. What is the office of the keys?

A. The preaching of the holy gospel and Christian discipline. By these two means the kingdom of heaven is opened to believers and shut against unbelievers.

Q.84. How is the kingdom of heaven opened and shut by the preaching of the holy gospel?

A. In this way: The kingdom of heaven is opened when it is proclaimed and openly testified to believers, one and all, according to the command of Christ, that as often as they accept the promise of the gospel with true faith all their sins are truly forgiven them by God for the sake of Christ's gracious work. On the contrary, the wrath of God and eternal condemnation fall upon all unbelievers and hypocrites as long as they do not repent. It is according to this witness of the gospel that God will judge the one and the other in this life and in the life to come.

Q.85. How is the kingdom of heaven shut and opened by Christian discipline?

A. In this way: Christ commanded that those who bear the Christian name in an unchristian way either in doctrine or in life should be given brotherly admonition. If they do not give up their errors or evil ways, notification is given to the church or to those ordained for this by the church. Then, if they do not change after this warning,they are forbidden to partake of the holy Sacraments and are thus excluded from the communion of the church and by God himself from the kingdom of Christ. However, if they promise and show real amendment, they are received again as members of Christ and of the church.

***The Heidelberg Catechism (HC)* [LORD'S DAY 51]**

Q.126. What is the fifth petition?

A. "And forgive us our debts, as we also have forgiven our debtors." That is:be pleased, for the sake of Christ's blood, not to charge to us, miserable sinners, our many transgressions, nor the evil which still clings to us. We also find this witness of thy grace in us, that it is our sincere intention heartily to forgive our neighbor (*BOC*, HC 4.126).

II. Westminster Shorter Catechism (WSC)

Q.105. What do we pray for in the fifth petition?

A. In the fifth petition, which is, "And forgive us our debts, as we forgive our debtors, "we pray that God, for Christ's sake, would freely pardon all our sins (Ps 51:1; Rom 3:24-25); *which we are the rather encouraged to ask because by his grace we are enabled from the heart to forgive others* (Luke 11:4; Matt 6:14-15; 18:35) (*BOC*, WSC 7.105).

III. Westminster Larger Catechism (WLC)

Q.194. What do we pray for in the fifth petition?

A. In the fifth petition (which is, "Forgive us our debts, as we forgive our debtors") (Matt 6:12), *acknowledging that we and all others are guilty both of original and actual sin, and thereby become debtors to the justice of God, and neither we nor any other creature can make the least satisfaction for that debt* (Matt 18:24; Rom 3:9, 19; 5:19; Ps 130:3; Mic 6:6-7): *we pray for ourselves and others, that God of his free grace would, through the obedience and satisfaction of Christ apprehended and applied by faith, acquit us both from the guilt and punishment of sin* (Rom 3:24-25; 5:19; Acts 13:39), *accept us in his Beloved* (Eph 1:6), *continue his favor and grace to us* (2Pet 1:2), *pardon our daily failings* (Hos 14:2; Ps 130:3; 143:2); *and fill us with peace and joy, in giving us daily more and more assurance of forgiveness* (Rom 5:1-2; 15:13; Ps 51:7-12), *which we are the rather emboldened to ask, and encouraged to expect, when we have this testimony in ourselves, that we from the heart forgive others their offenses* (Luke 11:4; Matt 6:14-15; 18:35) (*BOC*, WLC 7.304).

6. The Sixth Petition:

"And lead us not into temptation, but deliver us from evil" (Matthew 6:13)

καὶ μὴ εἰσενέγκῃς ἡμᾶς εἰς πειρασμόν
ἀλλὰ ῥῦσαι ἡμᾶς ἀπὸ τοῦ πονηροῦ

i. "lead us not into temptation." Like the fifth petition, the sixth takes a twofold, proverbial form. On the surface of it, however, while the latter part of this petition appears understandable and necessary, the first part is troubling. Why is it necessary to ask our heavenly Father to "lead us not into temptation"? In asking for such a thing, are we not assuming that it were actually possible? But is it not unthinkable that our God would participate in bringing about our temptation?

We have good reason for asking. In fact, *God does not tempt us.* After all, the apostle says, "No one, when tempted, should say, 'I am being tempted by God'; for God cannot be tempted by evil and he himself tempts no one" (Jas 1:13). We know that it is Satan, not God, who is the tempter (Matt 4:1-11; Mark 1:13; Luke 4:2-13). The devil, as the tempter, is not only the one who snatches away the seed that falls on the path (Luke 8:12; Mark 4:15), but is also apparently working to bring about the failure of those seeds that fall on the path, those that "have no root," who "believe only for a while and in a time of testing fall away" (Luke 8:13; Mark 4:16-17). Paul says it is because Satan had thwarted his attempts to visit the Thessalonians (1Thess 2:17-20) that he confessed his worry for them: "For this reason, when I could bear it no longer, I sent to find out about your faith; I was afraid that somehow the tempter had tempted you and that our labor had been in vain" (1Thess 3:5)

It is not at all easy to distinguish between tempting and testing in the New Testament, since the same root word is behind both. A complete understanding of what it involves, therefore, must recognize the testing Jesus endured, not only from the tempter, but also from the religious authorities (Matt 16:1; 19:3; 22:18, 35; Mark 8:11; 10:2; 12:15; Luke 11:16; 20:23; John 8:6), who at times may well have given voice, as Peter did on one occasion (Matt 16:21-23), to the evil one (Matt 16:4; Luke 11:17-26).

Further, the translation (NRSV) of the petition as we have it in both Matthew and Luke adds another, specifically juridical, dimension: "and do not bring us to the time of trial" (Matt 6:13a; Luke 11:4). Once again, we find ourselves in the midst of a potentially bewildering tension, trying to distinguish between the positive and negative, relative and absolute, qualitative and quantitative senses to this one root word variously rendered: *temptation*, *testing*, *trial.* If we may say with some certainty that God does not tempt us, as we have done by drawing an appropriate "infinite qualitative distinction" between God and Satan, how then do we measure what would seem to be a quantitative distinction, namely, the degree to which God allows testing, as in the first two chapters of Job (1:1-2:13)? Or, bearing in mind the legally qualitative distinction that exists between a judge and those over whom he has absolute authority to render a verdict, how are we to understand the petition that we not be brought to trial? In some ways, we have already answered the latter question in our consideration of the fifth petition, for we now realize that authority to forgive and the admonition to seek reconciliation within the sphere of human relations and relative indebtedness is in fact given to us. We are to be reconciled to our accusers before our cases get to trial (Matt 5:23-26). So let us set aside the latter question for the time being. We will return to it when we address the second part of this petition, namely, that we be rescued from the evil one. For now let us return to the quantitative question of God's role in allowing *testing*, *temptation*, and *trials*.

If we state it passively in this way, however, why this strange petition? Why ask that God *not* take an active role in leading us into temptation? The distinction lies between the idea of God's actively tempting us, which God does *not* do, and the possibility that God *may actively lead* us into, or *passively allow us* to enter periods and places where we are tested, tempted, or in a sense, put on trial by others. As a precedent for the latter, consider the synoptic accounts of Jesus' temptation in the wilderness: although Luke says the Spirit "led" Jesus "in" the wilderness (Luke 4:1); Matthew states the purpose for which the Spirit led Jesus into the wilderness was "to be tempted by the devil"

(4:1); meanwhile, Mark puts it most strongly: "the Spirit immediately drove him out into the wilderness" (1:12).

Additional testimony to God's active leading agency is found in Psalm 125:

> But those who turn aside to their own crooked ways
> the LORD will lead away with evildoers.
> Peace be upon Israel! (Ps 125:5)

We may further recall that, where Paul assured the Corinthian church that it was now time to forgive a controversial figure in that church and that he himself would forgive as they forgave and consoled the sinner — presumably the man who had been having sexual intercourse with his stepmother (1Cor 5:1-2) — what brought about his subsequent repentance and reconciliation was, at least in part, Paul's determination that they should "hand this man over to Satan for the destruction of the flesh, so that his spirit may be saved in the day of the Lord" (1Cor 5:5). Here is an example of the apostle taking an active role in consigning someone to the tempter, though, as with Psalm 125, the pattern of "turning aside to their own crooked ways" seems already to have been established. The activity of turning one over to Satan or leading away the evildoer could even be explained as a passive suspension of any active defense of their wicked conduct.

There is considerably more scriptural evidence, however, to support the latter, passive sense in which God *permits* us to be tested, or even the passive sense in which *we* may "*fall into* temptation" or "*be trapped by* many senseless and harmful desires that plunge people into ruin and destruction" (1Tim 6:9; italics mine).

As with the third petition (the last of the three *thy*-petitions), the sixth petition (the last of the *we*-petitions) also figures in the scene in the Garden of Gethsemane, where Jesus urges his drowsy and depressed disciples, Peter, James, and John, to stay awake and watch with him and to "pray that *you* may not come into the time of trial; the spirit indeed is willing, but the flesh is weak" (Matt 26:41; Mark 14:38). In fact, in Luke's account, Jesus admonishes the disciples not once, but twice (Luke 22:40, 46). Further, this double admonition frames a chiasm or a "sandwich" arrangement that reveals something interesting, a pattern that revolves around and focusses on the appearance of an angel to give him strength (cf. Mark 1:13) to endure in his time of temptation *in extremis*.

v. 40 When he reached the place, he said to them, "Pray that you may not come into the time of trial."

> v. 41 Then he withdrew from them about a stone's throw, knelt down, and prayed,
>
> > *v. 42 "Father, if you are willing, remove this cup from me; yet, not my will but yours be done."*
> >
> > > **v. 43 Then an angel from heaven appeared to him and gave him strength.**
> >
> > *v. 44 In his anguish he prayed more earnestly, and his sweat became like great drops of blood falling down on the ground.*
>
> v. 45 When he got up from prayer, he came to the disciples and found them sleeping because of grief,

v. 46 and he said to them, "Why are you sleeping? Get up and pray that you may not come into the time of trial."

As if the question of agency is not complex enough, Jesus couches this petition in such a way that the disciples are to ask that they themselves not be allowed to actively *come* to trial. Notice that Jesus has introduced two new terms, namely, the issue of the *will* and the dialectic of *strength and weakness*. Though his statement "the flesh is weak" apparently pertains to the disciples, it is possible that Jesus speaks of his own flesh as well, at least to the extent that the sending of an angel to strengthen him, or to strengthen his will, is deemed necessary. The temptation of Jesus is one matter, of course, ours is another.

Paul offers an encouraging word in this regard, which he also states quantitatively in terms of strength: "No testing has overtaken you that is not common to everyone. God is faithful, and he will not let you be tested beyond your strength, but with the testing he will also provide the way out so that you may be able to endure it" (1Cor 10:13). Here God passively allows the testing, but actively provides a way out, an escape route. Further, we are given the assurance that we are not alone in our trials. Our trials and temptations are "common to everyone" (cf. 1Pet 4:12). But we have the added — no, the qualitatively higher — assurance that the very Christ who was tempted in every way as we are, yet who remained with out sin (Heb 4:15), the same Christ who endured the cross, is with and in, among and for us, and therefore we should have every confidence in his ability to help us (Heb 2:18) when we encounter temptations, and we can take courage to face ourselves in the process of self-examination. Thus, Paul urges: "Examine yourselves to see whether you are living in the faith. Test yourselves. Do you not realize that Jesus Christ is in you? —unless, indeed, you fail to meet the test!" (2Cor 13:5).

This need for strength to endure in times of trial, when viewed in light of the promised presence of the Christ who endured the cross (Heb 12:2-3), reframes our quantitative need in terms that plainly show we do not lack what is qualitatively decisive in granting us the victory over temptation, namely, that which we have already asked for in the third petition; that which is extended to us in our hour of greatest need; that which, when we reach for it, comes to us with sufficient strengthening: *the will of God*. In fact, the will of God is *not* that we should be led into temptation, and that is why we are so instructed to pray what amounts to a negation of the thought. Rather, it is our own will that constitutes the problem. As we have noted above, God "himself tempts no one. But one is tempted *by one's own desire*, being lured and enticed by it" (Jas 1:13b-14; italics mine). Here again, we see a petition that clearly assumes, builds on, and reiterates what has gone before. To pray, "lead us not into temptation," is to say again, "thy will be done." It is to keep Christ's "word of patient endurance" as did the saints in Philadelphia; such steadfastness and perseverance is in turn the basis for the risen Christ's assurance to them: "Because you have kept my word of patient endurance, I will keep you from the hour of trial that is coming on the whole world to test the inhabitants of the earth" (Rev 3:10). Is such a hope to be dismissed as merely separatist, sectarian, gnostic escapism? Call it what you will, it does not dissuade Jesus from instructing us quite directly, even commanding us, to: "Be alert at all times, praying that you may have the strength to escape all these things that will take place, and to stand before the Son of Man" (Luke 21:36). But how many of us actually pray this way? Surely, this instruction occurs in Luke's apocalyptic chapter, but is our day and age any less apocalyptic than when Jesus issed this instruction?

It is assumed in The Lord's Prayer, and in many of the Lord's other teachings on prayer, that we should seek to avoid trials and temptations. Likewise, Paul urges us to avoid setting ourselves up or allowing ourselves to be lured into tempting situations (1Cor 7:5; Gal 6:1). Neither are we to harden our hearts "as in the rebellion, as on the day of testing in the wilderness." The stakes are enormously high! For those who rebelled against God, who were disobedient, "were unable to the enter (the promised land) because of unbelief" (Heb 3:7-19). Thus, we are told:

> Take care, brothers and sisters, that none of you may have an evil, unbelieving heart that turns away from the living God. But exhort one another every day, as long as it is called "today," so that none of you may be hardened by the deceitfulness of sin. For we have become partners of Christ, if only we hold our first confidence firm to the end (Heb 3:12-14).

Nevertheless, The Lord's Prayer is not unrealistic about the fact that temptations will arise, regardless of how we are led or lured into them, regardless of *how* they arise. We are not to seek them out. But scripture also promises us that, when they do arise, there is blessing and joy on the other side, for those who endure:

> My brothers and sisters, whenever you face trials of any kind, consider it nothing but joy. ... Blessed is anyone who endures temptation. Such a one has stood the test and will receive the crown of life that the Lord has promised to those who love him (Jas 1:1, 12).

> Blessed be the God and Father of our Lord Jesus Christ! By his great mercy he has given us a new birth into a living hope through the resurrection of Jesus Christ from the dead, and into an inheritance that is imperishable, undefiled, and unfading, kept in heaven for you, who are being protected by the power of God through faith for a salvation ready to be revealed in the last time. In this you rejoice, even if now for a little while you have had to suffer various trials, so that the genuineness of your faith - being more precious than gold that, though perishable, is tested by fire - may be found to result in praise and glory and honor when Jesus Christ is revealed (1Pet 1:3-7).

> Therefore, since we are surrounded by so great a cloud of witnesses, let us also lay aside every weight and the sin that clings so closely, and let us run with perseverance the race that is set before us, looking to Jesus the pioneer and perfecter of our faith, who for the sake of the joy that was set before him endured the cross, disregarding its shame, and has taken his seat at the right hand of the throne of God (Heb 12:1-2).

The latter reminder of the unsurpassed perseverance of Christ on the cross should remind us of the supreme Old Testament prefiguration of the cross, namely, the testing of Abraham and Isaac (Gen 22:1; Heb 11:17), which in turn suggests that, at Calvary, it is as much the Father who is being tested as the Son. Isaac is a figure of Christ the Son, but in Genesis, it is Abraham, Isaac's father, who is said to be tested (22:1). This in no way diminishes the severity of the test of the cross for Christ Jesus the Son, nor is it to suggest that the possibility of testing the Father is ever to enter our thinking. Quite to the contrary, it is precisely to warn us against any thought of testing God. While it is beyond the scope of our task to thoroughly consider the several stark admonitions that warn us: "Do not put the Lord your God to the test" (Luke 4:12), we should at least emphasize that such warnings are not only frequent in scripture (Acts 5:9; 15:10; *et al.*), but they also finally contain within them the terrible possibility that God may indeed, in the face of particularly stubborn rebellion, take an active role in leading away the evildoers (Ps 125:5; cf. 1:4-6).

***ii. "but deliver us from evil* (or *from the evil one*)."** In the Sermon on the Mount, the phrase is rendered: "but rescue us from the evil one" (Matt 6:13b). In Luke, the phrase is omitted altogether, indicating that the first half of the petition: "And do not bring us to the time of trial" (Luke 11:14b) expresses sufficiently what in Matthew constitutes a synonymous parallelism. In other words, there is a sense in which the phrase adds little to the petition, but simply restates it in reverse fashion. On the other hand, the second part of the parallelism makes it clear that the particular form of testing we seek to avoid is not any mundane annoyance that tries the patience, but evil itself, or the evil one: the tempter, the enemy, the devil, the accuser of the saints.

Considering how frequently the theme of rescue, deliverance, and salvation occur in scripture, it is somewhat surprising that the word in use here [ῥῦσαι] is relatively rare, meaning *to snatch away, tear up, dig out, set free,* or *liberate*. Further, the word is used to describe rescue from extreme threats, such as death (Matt 27:43), or "this body of death" in which the depravity of sin seems almost unavoidable and the human will itself seems perversely bound (Rom 7:24); other threats include the coming wrath (1Thess 1:10); the "power of darkness" (Col 1:13); enemies (Luke 1:74); and wicked and evil people (2Thess 3:2).

What may seem somewhat surprising, however, is that these "wicked and evil people" are explicitly characterized as such precisely for their lack of saving faith (2Thess 3:2). The coming of the Deliverer out of Zion will result in the banishment of ungodliness from Jacob (Rom 11:26). Paul hopes that he "may be rescued from the unbelievers in Judea" (Rom 15:31). Surprising it may be, but this accords with what we have said elsewhere when we stated that faith is the opposite of sin (Rom 14:23).[25] Faith saves, but "the wages of sin is death." Therefore, to be snatched from the evil one is to be delivered into an entirely new realm, delivered perhaps even in the same way that a child is delivered into a whole new world. It involves entrance into an altogether new sphere: "He has rescued us from the power of darkness and transferred us into the kingdom of his beloved Son, in whom we have redemption, the forgiveness of sins" (Col 1:13-14).

We should not miss the *desperate* nature of the situations with which this verb is associated. Three occurrences of this rare verb are clustered in one verse (2Cor 1:10) set in a passage that not only makes starkly clear the extreme sort of despair from which the apostle asked to be snatched, but also the crucial function that prayer served in bringing about the needed rescue:

> We do not want you to be unaware, brothers and sisters, of the affliction we experienced in Asia; for we were so utterly, unbearably crushed that we despaired of life itself. Indeed, we felt that we had received the sentence of death *so that we would rely not on ourselves but on God* who raises the dead He who *rescued* us from so deadly a peril will continue to *rescue* us; on him we have set our hope that he will *rescue* us again, *as you also join in helping us by your prayers*, so that many will give thanks on our behalf for the blessing granted us *through the prayers of many* (2Cor 1:8-11; italics mine).

When we pray to our heavenly Father, "deliver us from evil," we may be assured that we are relying on the One who alone continually rescues, for "the Lord knows how to rescue the godly from trial, and to keep the unrighteous under punishment until the day of judgment" (2Pet 2:9). More than that, we know that "Deliverance belongs to the LORD!" These are the very words that spew from the mouth of Jonah as he in turn is spewed from the mouth of the great fish (2:9; Ps 3:8). Just as our rescue issues in praise of the One to whom deliverance belongs, so too our very cries for help can glorify our deliverer: "I cried aloud to him, and he was extolled with my tongue" (Ps 66:17). Ultimately, then, this petition and all the petitions that together make up The Lord's Prayer are words of praise. In fact, one has the impression that, in many ways, the six petitions are really one petition after all, one petition spoken in six different ways. With this in mind, let us turn to the doxological conclusion of the prayer, and in doing so, bring our discussion to a close.

I. The Heidelberg Catechism (HC) [LORD'S DAY 52]

Q.127. What is the sixth petition?

A. "And lead us not into temptation, but deliver us from evil." That is: since we are so weak that we cannot stand by ourselves for one moment, and besides, since our sworn enemies, the devil, the world, and our own sin, ceaselessly assail us, be pleased to preserve and strengthen us through the power of thy Holy Spirit so that we may stand firm against them, and not be defeated in this spiritual warfare, until at last we obtain complete victory (*BOC*, HC 4.127).

II. Westminster Shorter Catechism (WSC)

Q.106. What do we pray for in the sixth petition?

A. In the sixth petition, which is, "And lead us not into temptation, but deliver us from evil," we pray that God would either keep us from being tempted to sin (Matt 26:41; Ps 19:13) *or support and deliver us when we are tempted* (1Cor 10:13; Ps 51:10, 12) (*BOC*, WSC 7.106).

III. Westminster Larger Catechism (WLC)

Q.195. What do we pray for in the sixth petition?

A. In the sixth petition (which is, "And lead us not into temptation, but deliver us from evil") (Matt 6:13), *acknowledging that the most wise, righteous, and gracious God, for divers holy and just ends, may so order things that we may be assaulted, foiled, nd for a time led captive by temptations* (2Chron 32:31; Job 2:6); *that Satan* (1Pet 5:8; Job 2:2), *the world* (Luke 21:34; Mark 4:19), *and the flesh, are ready powerfully to draw us aside and ensnare us* (Jas 1:14); *and that we, even after the pardon of our sins, by reason of our corruption* (Gal 5:17; Rom 7:18), *weakness, and want of watchfulness* (Matt 26:41), *are not only subject to be tempted, and forward to expose ourselves unto temptations* (1Tim 6:9; Prov 7:22), *but also of ouselves unable and unwilling to resist them, to recover out of them, and to improve them* (Rom 7:18-19); *and worthy to be left under the power of them* (Ps 81:11-12); *we pray: that God would so overrule the world and all in it* (John 17:15; Rom 8:28), *subdue the flesh* (Ps 51:10; 119:133), *and restrain Satan* (Heb 2:18; 1Cor 10:13; 2Cor 12:8), *order all things* (Rom 8:28), *bestow and bless all means of grace* (Heb 13:20-21; Eph 4:11-12), *and quicken us to watchfulness in the use of them, that we and all his people may by his providence be kept from being tempted to sin* (Heb 13:20-21; Eph 4:11-12); *or, if tempted, that by his Spirit we may be powerfully supported and enabled to stand in the hour of temptation* (1Cor 10:13; Eph 3:14-16); *or, when fallen, raised again and recovered out of it* (Ps 51:12), *and have a sanctified use and improvement thereof* (1Pet 1:6-7; 5:10); *that our sanctification and salvation may be perfected* (1Thess 3:13), *Satan trodden under our feet* (Rom 16:20), *and we fully freed from sin, temptation, and all evil forever* (1Thess 5:23) (*BOC*, WLC 7.305).

Conclusion

DOXOLOGY:

[***For Thine is the Kingdom and the Power and the Glory forever! Amen.***] (Matthew 6:13b)

[Ὅτι σοῦ ἐστιν ἡ βασιλεία καὶ ἡ δύναμις καὶ ἡ δόξα
εἰς τοὺς αἰῶνας. Ἀμήν.]

The threefold *doxology*, or *ascription of praise*, is not found in most early manuscripts, but this does not necessarily suggest an intrusion. On the contrary, as Luz states, that the twofold ascription as found in the Didache (8:2) — *"yours is the power and the glory forever"* — indicates "the Lord's Prayer was prayed in the Greek church from the beginning with a doxology." Luz further observes that "Jewish prayers ... without a concluding doxology are unthinkable."[26] This is true not only in corporate worship, but also private prayers as well.[27]

Regarding the latter, Paul's final word of testimony and instruction to Timothy not only attaches such a doxology to the conclusion of his correspondence, but also evinces much of what we have learned in our study of The Lord's Prayer. In three short verses, Paul's "last will and testament" speaks of forgiveness, the strengthening of the will, the preaching the gospel, rescue from evil, the heavenly kingdom of the Lord, all of which Paul seals with praise:

> At my first defense no one came to my support, but all deserted me. *May it not be counted against them!* But *the Lord stood by me and gave me strength*, so that through me *the message might be fully proclaimed* and all the Gentiles might hear it. So I was *rescued* from the lion's mouth. *The Lord will rescue me from every evil attack and save me for his heavenly kingdom. To him be the glory forever and ever. Amen* (2Tim 4:16-18).

With respect to corporate worship, scholars point with near unanimity to David's final prayer, spoken at the dedication of the offerings for the building at the temple:

> Then David blessed the LORD in the presence of all the assembly; David said: "Blessed are you, O LORD, the God of our ancestor Israel, forever and ever. Yours, O LORD, are the greatness, the power, the glory, the victory, and the majesty; for all that is in the heavens and on the earth is yours; yours is the Kingdom, O LORD, and you are exalted as head above all. Riches and honor come from you, and you rule over all. In your hand are power and might; and it is in your hand to make great and to give strength to all. And now, our God, we give thanks to you and praise your glorious name" (1Chron 29:10-13).

Not surprisingly, while the earliest manuscripts show considerable variety and freedom at this very point, that is, in their diverse renderings of the doxology, we also find well over a dozen sources adding, after the word *glory*, the Trinitarian attribution: "*of the Father, and of the Son, and of the Holy Spirit.*" While these are generally late sources, this underscores the point we made in our introduction and recalled at various stages in these studies, namely, that for centuries Christians have seen in The Lord's Prayer strong affinity and even structural coherence with the doctrine of the Trinity. Thus, we are free to say, for instance, that our Father's kingdom is the holy kingdom wherein "the name" is hallowed; the power of Christ Jesus the Son is that which strengthens and nourishes us to do God's will; and the glory of the Holy Spirit is evident wherever sins are forgiven and debts are cancelled, and wherever victory over evil is granted by means of rescue from imminent danger. Nevertheless, as with the doctrine of the Trinity, there is overlap and agreement, harmony and unity, between the divine persons. The Son who is "seated at the right hand of power" (Matt 26:64) is as much King as the Father, and as much responsible for the grace of forgiveness as the Spirit. Likewise, we may say that the Spirit is as much the "power source" as the Father and the Son. Thus, we can affirm the doxological conclusion contained in so many of the prayers in such resources as the *Book of Common Worship* of the PC(USA). In sealing our prayers with, or asking "in the name" of "*Jesus Christ our Lord,*" it is appropriate that we continue, "*who lives and reigns with you and the Holy Spirit, one God, now and forever. Amen.*"

What is regrettable in this (in most respects) monumental resource, is that so many of its eucharistic prayers—even when

Trinitarian in intent—address the First Person of the Trinity generically as "God," without specific reference to "the Father." In its efforts at gender-inclusive language for God and quite despite its affirmation of the co-regency of Christ and the unity of the Godhead, such formulations infer that the Son of God and the Holy Spirit are *not* God, and obscure the metaphor of the divine Father-Son relation by mentioning only "half" the relation, so to speak.

I mention this, not to add fuel to inclusive language debates or to trumpet a supposedly superior masculinity or an engendered understanding of God, but to call attention to the need to preserve and think through the metaphors as we have them in scripture for all their frequently unexplored and revelatory richness, which is quickly lost when these metaphors are forced to reflect what we assume are ideal human relationships and not what God has elected to reveal of God's relational nature at a patriarchal epoch of history.

This is borne out in one final doxology that we do well to consider with due eschatological alertness and prayerful sobriety:

> The end of all things is near; therefore be serious and discipline yourselves *for the sake of your prayers*. ... Whoever speaks must do so *as one speaking the very words of God*; whoever serves must do so with *the strength that God supplies, so that God may be glorified in all things through Jesus Christ. To him belong the glory and the power forever and ever. Amen* (1Pet 4:7, 11).

Here again, the momentum of the apostle's admonition builds toward the *telos* of the power and glory of God through Christ, yet it begins with conforming ourselves to the will and intention of God in Christ. In other words, this is neither an assertion of rights and privileges, nor a claim to equality and entitlements. On the contrary, I am told to discipline myself for the sake of my prayers (the effectiveness of which I am given no reason to doubt), and to align my prayer entirely with the will of God: "Since therefore Christ suffered in the flesh, arm yourselves also with the same intention (for whoever has suffered in the flesh has finished with sin), so as to live for the rest of your earthly life no longer by human desires but by the will of God" (1Pet 4:1-2).

Admittedly, this particular passage does not speak of God as "the Father," but neither does it speak explicitly of Christ Jesus as "the Son," that is, not at this precise point. But this does not discount the general rule that where mentioned is made of the Son, it is in the Son's specific relation to the Father. We do not digress, because, as we have been continually reminded throughout these studies, we are addressing our Father, as we have been instructed to do so by Christ Jesus the Son, and the whole of The Lord's Prayer is to be understood as precisely this sort of intimate and familiar, loving and reverent, grateful and respectful, appeal. Indeed, as this is *the Lord's* prayer, each time we offer it we do so in *imitation* of Christ Jesus the Son and we can trust that we are also brought ever more into conformity with his image: "For those whom he foreknew he also predestined to be conformed to the image of his Son, in order that he might be the firstborn within a large family" (Rom 8:29). *Those who pray thus to "Our heavenly father," in grateful acknowledgment of the Father's gift of the Son* (John 3:16-17) *may say with confidence, "We are that family!"* In other words, when we pray the prayer that Jesus taught we do, in fact, "let the same mind be in (us) that was in Christ Jesus" (Phil 2:5); we are allowing his Lordship, his kingdom, his will to exercise authority over us for our personal transformation (Rom 12:2) into his image, and our communal transformation into his body, his family, his church, his bride.

ﻌ

I. The Heidelberg Catechism (HC) [LORD'S DAY 52]

Q.128. How do you close this prayer?

A. "For thine is the kingdom and the power and the glory, forever." That is: we ask all this of thee because, as our King, thou art willing and able to give us all that is good since thou hast power over all things, and that by this not we ourselves but thy holy name may be glorified forever (*BOC*, HC 4.128).

Q.129. What is the meaning of the little word "Amen"?

A. Amen means:this shall truly and certainly be. For my prayer is much more certainly heard by God than I am persuaded in my heart that I desire such things from him (*BOC*, HC 4.129).

ﻌ

II. Westminster Shorter Catechism (WSC)

Q.107. What doth the conclusion of the Lord's Prayer teach us?

A. The conclusion of the Lord's Prayer, which is, "For thine is the kingdom,and the power, and the glory, forever; Amen," teacheth us to take our encouragement in prayer from God only (Dan 9:18-19), *and in our prayers to praise him, ascribing Kingdom, power, and glory to him* (1Chron 29:11-13); *and in testimony of our desire and assurance to be heard, we say, "Amen"* (Rev 22:20-21; 1Cor 14:16) (*BOC*, WSC 7.107).

***III. Westminster Larger Catechism* (WLC)**

Q.196. What doth the conclusion of the Lord's Prayer teach us?

A. The conclusion of the Lord's Prayer (which is, "For thine is the Kingdom, and the power, and the glory, for ever. Amen,") (Matt 6:13), *teacheth us to enforce our petitions with arguments* (Job 23:3-4; Jer 14:20-21), *which are to be taken, not from any worthiness in ourselves, or in any other creature, but from God* (Dan 9:4, 7-9, 16, 19), *and with our prayers to join praises* (Phil 4:6), *ascribing to God alone eternal sovereignty, omnipotency, and glorious excellency* (1Chron 29:10-13); *in regard whereof, as he is able and willing to help us* (Eph 3:20-21; Luke 11:13; Ps 84:11), *so we by faith are emboldened to plead with him that he would* (Eph 3:12; Heb 10:19-22), *and quietly to rely upon him that he will, fulfill our requests* (1John 5:14; Rom 8:32). *And to testify our desires and assurance, we say, "Amen"* (1Cor 14:16; Rev 22:20-21) (*BOC*, WLC 7.306).

An Eschatological Postscript

As we have seen in the course of this study, and as one will discover in any thorough exposition "the Prayer," we have direct instruction from the Lord Jesus Christ to offer certain other specific petitions for which comparatively few believers pray. Still less are these petitions regular features of the church's liturgy, as is The Lord's Prayer. Consider, for instance, the missional instruction to ask the Lord of the harvest to send out laborers into the harvest (Matt 9:37-38; Luke 10:2). There are no qualifiers attached to that direction which mitigate its importance or suggest it is for only occassional use. Rather, as we have seen in our consideration of the fourth petition (especially as we have read it in light of John 4:34-38), such a petition should be expressed often, even daily, for it carries no less urgency than our need for regular sustanance, it clearly accords with the will of God, it enlists the resources of God's household for the fulfillment of the Great Commission, it lightens our personal burdens, and it promises the eschatological hope of treasure in heaven.

Perhaps more obscure, but no less important in these apocalyptic times, is the admonition to pray for those living in Judea who will be forced to flee to the mountains when "the desolating sacrilege is set up where it ought not to be;" that is, to pray that their "flight may not be in winter or on the Sabbath." (Matt 24:15-25) How many Christians living today ever think to pray for this? I suspect very few do so, since it seems to concern a time, a place, a people, and a situation far removed from the church in the west.

These are just two examples from the broader teachings of Jesus on prayer that I would suggest invite a suspension of disbelief, more serious consideration, and far more frequent use. Whether or not they may be considered on a par with the petitions of the Lord's Prayer is not a matter to be adjudicated here, since their comparative neglect cannot be disputed. With the aim of correcting that imbalance then, however slightly, I offer the following prayer, adapted from those (mostly synoptic) gospel texts in which the Lord offers direct and explicit instruction with respect to prayer, and supplies their specific content. (Surprisingly, the words *pray*, *prays*, *prayed*, *prayer*, *praying*, do not occur in the *NRSV* translation of the Gospel of John, no doubt since nearly every word of Jesus in John is permeated with prayer.) In the interest then of, shall we say, experimental obedience, I invite and urge the reader to appropriate, adapt if needed, and pray often, perhaps daily for a season, the following prayer and share it with trusted believers, adding it to, but not replacing, the regular daily offering of The Lord's Prayer.

Our heavenly Father, who hears in secret,
hear this secret prayer:
    for insofar as I believe, I know I will receive,
    and insofar as I believe you, I know I will receive you,
    you who alone are good,
    you who are always quick to open heaven
        and give us your Holy Spirit without measure.

For all who are oppressed by unclean spirits,
    or deceived by the father of lies,
    or blinded by guides who are themselves blind,
    or crippled in their faith by hypocrites,
    for all who have stumbled over doubts and heresies,
    for all who simply await the good news,
    hear our petitions and act swiftly, we pray:

Send forth laborers into your harvest,
    silence and bind, rebuke and expel the enemy,
    supply the need of the naked and the lost,
    that they might be clothed
    and found in their right minds
    and join us in worshipping you in spirit and in truth!

But where your answers seem slow to us,
    let us not be discouraged or disheartened,
    neither let our faith ever fail us
    — for Christ is our faith! —
    but help us to strengthen our fellow believers.

May this prayer never be as empty phrases before you,
    neither let it be heard in accusation of any,
    nor let it be offered for the sake of appearance,
    but receive it as our declaration of forgiveness
        of all who have harmed or hurt or wronged us.

Rather, bless those who curse us,
    excuse those who abuse us,
    reward (according to your will and wisdom)
    those who persecute us,
    and fill us with love for our enemies,
    all that we might not come to the time of trial,
        or be led into temptation or the condemnation of others,
    for though the spirit is willing, the flesh is weak.

God, be merciful to me, a sinner!

Thank you, O Lord, that for the sake of your elect,
    you have cut short the last days
    in which the desolating sacrilege will be set up,
    and those who are in Judea shall flee to the mountains.
May their flight not be in winter or on a sabbath,
    but grant refuge to the refugee
    and wing to the weary.

But respecting all the troublesome things
that are to come before the consummation,
    give us vigilance and strength to escape
    the catastrophes, cataclysms, and convulsions of this age,
    and to stand before the Son of Man,
    himself the Son of God,
    Christ Jesus, our Savior and Lord.

Amen.

Notes

---

[1] *The Constitution of the Presbyterian Church (USA), Part I — The Book of*

[2] The complete series is also available online at Christian Classics Ethereal Library (www.ccel.org), and Project Canterbury (anglicanhistory.org), both accessed March 1, 2016).

[3] Available from Google Books at: https://books.google.com/books/about/A_body_of_practical_divinity_consisting.html?id=Mj5WAAAAcAAJ (accessed March 2, 2016).

[4] Also available online at: http://wesley.nnu.edu/john-wesley/the-sermons-of-john-wesley-1872-edition/sermon-26-upon-our-lords-sermon-on-the-mount-discourse-six (accessed March 1, 2016).

[5] Also available online at: http://www.gutenberg.org/files/34736/34736-h/34736-h.html#toc251 (accessed March 1, 2016).

[6] "The Didache" (8:1-2), in *The Apostolic Fathers, Second Edition*, trans. by J. B. Lightfoot and J. R. Harmer; ed. Michael W. Holmes (Grand Rapids: Baker Books, 1956), 246-249; esp. 258-259.

[7] Ulrich Luz, *Matthew 1-7: A Commentary*, trans. by Wilhelm C. Linss (Minneapolis: Augsburg, 1989) 372-73; Luz cites Cyprian (9 and 35) and Augustine, *City of God* (21:27).

[8] Ibid 372; Luz cites Tertullian (1)

[9] The following outline is a simplified version of that proposed by Luz.

[10] Herbert Lockyer, *All the Prayers of the Bible* (Grand Rapids: Zondervan, 1959) 192; cf. F. J. Burgess and D. B. Proudlove, *Watching unto Prayer: One Hundred Bible Readings on Prayer* (London: Lutterworth Press, 1944).

[11] Per Don Saliers, Barth's view of the Lord's Prayer stands in continuity with the Reformers, as well as the church fathers (Tertullian and Cyprian), who regarded it as part of the *traditio* taught to the newly baptized. See Saliers, "Introduction," in Karl Barth, *Prayer: 50th Anniv. Ed.* (Louisville: WJK, 2002) xii.

[12] Luz, 375.

[13] "This statement is based on the absence of any command to pray for the dead, and any example in the Scriptures of such prayer" (*BOC*, WLC 7.293, n. 9). No doubt the indulgence controversies which figured prominently in

precipitating the European Reformations are very much in the minds of the Westminster divines here. This strong prohibition against prayers for the dead, however, should not exclude the prayers of committal in the funeral rite, which have always, except for the strictest Puritans, served an important pastoral function.

[14] *Luther's Works (LW),* 43:200; cf. Luz, 374; n. 44.

[15] Luz, 374; n. 46.

[16] A. J. Worlledge, *Prayer: Oxford Library of Practical Theology, Second Edition* (London, New York, Bombay: Longmans, Green, and Co., 1902), 87.

[17] E.g., in the NRSV, *holy* occurs 630 times, *holiness* 29, *holiday* 4, *holies* 2, *hallow(ed)* 6; the various forms of *sanctif-y, -ying, -ied, -ication* 70 times; *consecrat-e, -es, -ed, -ing, -ion* 80 times.

[18] David P. Wright, "Molech," in *Harper Collins Bible Dictionary*, 694.

[19] Ibid.

[20] In Christian theology, the doctrine of the two kingdoms has been treated with such considerable variation and complexity that we cannot attempt to summarize or do justice to it here; suffice it to say it received perhaps its first important treatment by Augustine in *City of God,* where the two "cities" of Rome and the New Jerusalem are contrasted at length. Luther and Calvin each advanced a doctrine of the two kingdoms, these being, however, on the other side of the question of salvation. Both were concerned to set forth a clear understanding of the Christian society. For Calvin, the primary contrast lies between the eternal, spiritual and the temporal, political kingdoms. Meanwhile, such a worldview seems to underlie the parable of the good Samaritan, namely, in the contrast between Jerusalem and Jericho (Luke 10:30).

[21] Cornelio Fabro has identified a passage in Søren Kierkegaard's *Journals and Papers II* (1251), in which Kierkegaard resolves the tension between God's omnipotence and human freedom, as the most important page of writing from the 19th century.

[22] Luz, 381; n. 80.

[23] Georg Strecker and O. C. Dean, Jr., *The Sermon on the Mount: An Exegetical Commentary* (Edinburgh: T&T CLark, 1998).

[24] I have considered this metaphor at some length in "*Synkrinesis* as Following in Faith: Interpretation for a Kerygmatic Homiletic," in *Koinonia, Vol. XIII.2* (Fall 2001); 185-210.

[25] This is one of the essential premisses behind Kierkegaard's *Sickness Unto Death.*

[26] Luz, 385.

[27] Ibid.

Scripture Index

About the Author

TIMOTHY MATTHEW SLEMMONS is *Associate Professor of Homiletics and Worship* at the University of Dubuque Theological Seminary. A Presbyterian teaching elder, he has served churches in Pennsylvania and New Jersey, and preached as far afield as Jamaica, Scotland, and Malawi. A past recipient of the David H. C. Read Preacher/Scholar Award (1994), his publications include *Groans of the Spirit: Homiletical Dialectics in an Age of Confusion* (2010); *Year D: A Quadrennial Supplement to the Revised Common Lectionary* (2012); the 4-volume series, *Liturgical Elements for Reformed Worship* (2013-14); and *The Freedom of Christ: Sermons on Galatians* (2015).

Made in the USA
Middletown, DE
30 January 2020